PADUCAH AND THE CIVIL WAR

PADUCAH AND THE CIVIL WAR

JOHN PHILIP CASHON

THE History PRESS

Published by The History Press
Charleston, SC
www.historypress.net

First published 2016

Manufactured in the United States

ISBN 978.1.46713.696.9

Library of Congress Control Number: 2016941440

To my beautiful wife, who has shown me nothing but kindness and love while I struggled to follow my dream of writing, and her understanding the promise that I made to my father before he passed to keep fighting for my goal of becoming a published historian. Thank you, my love. I would also like to thank my family and friends for all of their ideas and feedback while writing this book.

Contents

Foreword

Much like the anticipation of Christmas is John's book of Paducah and the Civil War. Finally, there is an updated read that truly tells of the Union's importance of the occupation of Paducah and a detailed account of the Battle of Paducah. It is a revelation and, I hope, an eye opener for those who say nothing happened of importance in Paducah, Kentucky. Thank you, John, and I look forward to your next publication.

—John T. Suttles,
Commander, Kentucky Division,
Sons of Confederate Veterans

Preface

The goal of this book is to assist future historians and history enthusiasts by helping to remember the significance of Paducah in the Civil War and the role that it played. Paducah became the gateway into the Confederacy for the Union in the west, and it can be argued that the taking of Paducah was the single most important move that Grant did during the war. Holding Paducah opened the Tennessee River—and also the Cumberland River, due to its proximity—to all future movements deep into the South, and it enabled the Union to maintain supply lines deep into the Southern states. Without Grant taking Paducah, the war in the west may have been very different, and victory for the Union may not have occurred.

Most histories of the Civil War revolve around Lee's battles in the east, but it was in the west where there was not a stalemate. It is the mission of this book to highlight the role of Paducah, Kentucky, in the Western Theater of Operations.

Acknowledgements

I would like to thank Bill Baxter at the Lloyd Tilghman House and Civil War Museum and John Suttles, the Kentucky Division Commander of the Sons of Confederate Veterans, for all of the help they provided me with research materials and friendly support. Without them, this book would not have been possible. I would also like to acknowledge the Jackson Purchase Historical Society because its research materials were always available for me to delve into to find that one piece of information that I needed. Lastly, I would like to thank Mary Hammond with the Paducah Convention & Visitors Bureau for pointing me in the right direction whenever I felt stuck and needed help.

Chapter 1

Calls to Secede

Before the War of the Rebellion, 1818–60

To begin to understand the story of Paducah in the Civil War, one needs to envision the city before the war in regards to the early Jacksonian Democratic voting patterns in the Jackson Purchase and, later, the rise of the influence of Henry Clay's Whig Party in McCracken County and Paducah, where the rest of the Purchase remained heavily Democrat.

In 1818, almost ten years before Paducah became a town, the Jackson Purchase treaty with the Chickasaw Indians was completed. Because most of the early settlers into the region came from the southern states of North Carolina, South Carolina, Virginia, Georgia and Tennessee, they had a strong affinity for southerner Andrew "Old Hickory" Jackson, who lived in Nashville, Tennessee, which was much closer to them than Frankfort, Kentucky, which had leaders like Henry Clay. Because the Jackson Purchase was geographically isolated from the rest of Kentucky due to its being located west of the Tennessee River, the culture remained southern and strongly Democratic. In fact, the region was so Democratic that it was known as the "Democratic Gibraltar" of the state.[1]

When the 1824 presidential election took place, candidate Andrew Jackson was a heavy favorite in the Jackson Purchase, among other national candidates John Quincy Adams, Henry Clay and William H. Crawford. While 72.8 percent of Kentuckians voted for Henry Clay, Andrew Jackson controlled the votes in the Purchase, with Calloway County reporting 76.6

Henry Clay. *Library of Congress.*

percent, Hickman County reporting 68.4 percent and Graves County reporting 59 percent. Even though Andrew Jackson won the popular vote, as well as a larger number of electoral votes, he did not receive a majority of the electoral votes, which sent the decision to the Speaker of the House, Henry Clay, who chose John Quincy Adams; it was discovered later that a deal had been struck between the two where Henry Clay was appointed secretary of state by Adams. Many in the Jackson Purchase felt that their vote was stolen from them—and by another Kentuckian as well. This was not forgotten by many for years to come. In the 1828 presidential election, Andrew Jackson won convincingly, and in the Purchase, he received 90.5 percent in Calloway County, 80 percent in both Graves and Hickman Counties and 74 percent in the new county of McCracken.[2]

The national and state elections in the 1830s and 1840s continued the trend, as the Jackson Purchase counties voted for the Democratic Party. However, by 1836, McCracken County and Paducah had begun casting more votes for Henry Clay's Whig Party—McCracken County reported 58.4 percent of the votes for the unsuccessful candidate William Henry Harrison. This change in voting patterns can be attributed to the rise of the Roman Catholic, Jewish and northern-born residents who began to settle down the Ohio River in Paducah, as these residents brought a moderating influence by their having lived in the northern states. The German Jewish population began to immigrate to the United States due to the 1848 European revolutions, and many of these German immigrants became community leaders and established merchants in Paducah.[3]

Even though the 1820 Missouri Compromise helped diffuse arguments between the slaveholding and non-slaveholding states regarding the westward expansion of the United States, both the Northern Whigs and the Southern Democrats did not want to upset the balance between the free and slave states when California requested to join the Union as a free state in

Andrew Jackson. *Library of Congress.*

1849. The Compromise of 1850 was a set of national legislative laws, introduced by Henry Clay, to attempt to appease both sides. The compromise included measures to admit California as a free state; compensate Texas with $10 million if it would give up its boundary dispute with New Mexico; and create the Utah and New Mexico territories, where popular sovereignty allowed the inhabitants to choose whether there would be slavery or not. It made it easier for southerners to recover fugitive slaves with the Fugitive Slave Act, which forced northern abolitionists to hand over fugitive slaves under penalty of law, and it also ended the slave trade in Washington, D.C., even though it allowed slavery to continue in the capital. When the Kansas-Nebraska Act was passed in 1854, the Missouri Compromise was thoroughly repealed, and with the prospect of the transcontinental railroad in the West, the power struggle between free and slave state advocates kept the two from being able to find any future compromises.[4]

John Quincy Adams. *Library of Congress.*

One of the effects of the Compromise of 1850 was to ensure the future demise of the Whig Party, as the Northern Whigs and Southern Whigs were split by cultural and economic differences that were too much for them to overcome. The popular sovereignty clause was especially feared by the antislavery advocates in the Whig Party, as well as the Fugitive Slave Law, and by 1852, the Whig Party had become hopelessly divided. By 1854, with the passage of the Kansas-Nebraska Act, the Republican Party had formed and included members of the Northern Whigs and Free-Soil Party. The Whigs who favored slavery either joined the American (Know-Nothing) Party or switched over to the Democratic Party.[5]

On October 16, 1859, John Brown led a raid on the federal arsenal at Harpers Ferry, Virginia. His plan was to arm slaves with the weapons that were seized

John Brown. *Library of Congress.*

in the raid and create a slave revolt. Marines led by Robert E. Lee, local farmers and militiamen were able attack Brown's men and stop them from continuing with their plans. Regarding this raid, Quintus Quincy Quigley, a distinguished lawyer in Paducah who had been a staunch member of the Whig Party, noted in his journal, "Though I have but little fear of such a scheme ever maturing to any extent yet the fanaticism manifested by these men and the encouragement they received by men in high positions under cover evidences a spirit and a devotion to the cause of abolition which precludes the idea of the question ever being set at rest in the North." Quigley prophetically added, "What will be the developments of a few years almost makes the Patriot heart shutter [*sic*]…Each of the glorious stars in our heraldic flag might become separate sovereignties and upon the soil of each might and in many undoubtedly would be enacted scenes of carnage and blood that would cover up Napoleon's last great fields."[6]

Quigley lamented the end of the Whig Party in his journal on Saturday, December 24, 1859: "My political faith has always been that of the Whig but when with the expiring genius of Clay that party fell to pieces I attached myself to the American Party…But there lives and lingers in my mind a respect for and a belief in the principles of that glorious and imperial old Whig party that fades not nor loses its power though she is fallen."[7]

THE ELECTION OF 1860

The election of 1860 in the Jackson Purchase and Paducah followed the same patterns as earlier elections, in which the Democrats won more votes,

Clockwise from top left: Honorable John C. Breckinridge. Stephen A. Douglas. Abraham Lincoln. Honorable John Bell. *Library of Congress.*

except for McCracken County, which favored the Constitutional Union Party, in which members of the American Party typically united, though in this election there were divisions. The Democratic Party was divided by northern elements that favored popular sovereignty in the new western territories and southern elements that favored slavery to be allowed in those territories. The northern Democrat Stephen Douglas, who continued fighting for the Compromise of 1850 after Henry Clay became too sick to continue and also pushed for the Kansas-Nebraska Act, believed that the problems of slavery in the country were between the northern abolitionists and the southern disunionists. He favored preserving the Union by finding a middle ground. The southern Democrat nominee was John C. Breckinridge. The old northern Whigs became the Republican Party, which nominated Abraham Lincoln, and the old southern Whigs became the Constitutional Union Party, which nominated John Bell.

When the election results were finalized, the Jackson Purchase heavily favored John C. Breckinridge, with the exception of McCracken, but Ballard and Fulton Counties were very close. Ballard went for Bell with 39.9 percent, compared to Breckinridge receiving 37.5 percent. Fulton was 43.0 percent for Breckinridge and 42.0 percent for Bell, while McCracken County went heavily for Bell with 57.2 percent compared to Breckinridge's 19.7 percent. The votes for Douglas and Lincoln were inconsequential—Douglas received a small percentage of the vote, and Lincoln only received ten votes within the entire Jackson Purchase.[8]

DECEMBER 1860–AUGUST 1861

The Jackson Purchase, because of its southern roots, was shown from the 1860 presidential election results to be intensely southern in sympathy, as opposed to the rest of Kentucky, which had northern sympathies. When South Carolina seceded from the Union, the region became known as the "South Carolina of Kentucky."[9]

It was December 20, 1860, when South Carolina seceded from the Union, and in Paducah, this brought the differences to the forefront between the unionists and the pro-secessionists. On December 24, 1860, many of the citizens gathered at Gardner Hall, and Quintus Quigley described the meeting as being held "for the purpose of taking some action in relation to the state of the country for the preservation of the Union if possible and to give our weight in one direction or another." Quigley noticed that the meeting was "fast going over to dissolution," and he was "not prepared for the ultra-Southern ground and defiance breathed by the resolutions."[10]

The next day, on December 25, 1860, Quigley noted, "The first thing that arrested my attention in coming to my office was an effigy hung by the neck to the telegraph wire at the corner of Broadway and Locust Street with a large card attached inscribed 'the fate of a disunitionist.' The figure also had a copy of the Paducah Herald in its hand and the effigy was said to represent J.C. Noble, its Editor. After a short time the mayor had it taken down and then the boys put it on a dray and hauled it up and down the streets and finally in front of Noble's office on Main and then burned it."[11]

As more states began to secede after South Carolina, R.B.J. Twynam, a Democrat and the editor of the *Paducah Democrat* newspaper, pointed out that after the secession of South Carolina, "there were not half a dozen out-spoken secessionists in Paducah, but as State after State went out and took their stand by the side of South Carolina, the secession element gained strength, and one by one the people turned over to the side of the Southern Confederacy."[12]

On April 12, 1861, Fort Sumter was attacked by the Confederates in South Carolina, and many residents of Paducah lit lanterns to hang on their gates as tokens of support. Even though he wished to avert a Civil War, Quintus Quigley, like many of the other residents of Paducah, found

The Rziha map of Paducah—Broadway and Locust Street can be seen where Quigley said the effigy was hanging. *Wikimedia Commons.*

that he also began to support the Southern cause when he stated, "May the giver of all things avert the calamities of Civil War and incline the hearts and minds of men to settle this matter without blood but if in his unfortunate ordering conflict must come then my prayers are for the noble and gallant sons of the South."[13]

President Lincoln responded to South Carolina's attack on Fort Sumter on April 15, 1861, by requesting that each state in the Union raise seventy-five thousand volunteers to fight against the Confederacy. Quigley noted that the call for volunteers "spread like leaping flames over our city, and the same day saw us no longer divided but all united in rejecting him and his government and for support of the South. Our city grew wild and paraded out formations of companies and hallowing have filled up the town." Quigley continued, "Flags with 15 stars were raised and now float over the city."[14]

At the end of April 1861, the residents of Paducah learned that the Union army had moved into Cairo, Illinois, across the river at the confluence of the Ohio and Mississippi Rivers, and John C. Noble wrote in his *Paducah Herald* newspaper, "To Arms! To Arms!!…in God's name let it be done. It is disgraceful to Kentucky and to the South to suffer these vandals to quietly plunder our commerce."[15]

Not everyone wanted to rush to arms against the Federal government. Colonel Lloyd Tilghman of Paducah, the commander of the western division of the Kentucky Militia, including Paducah and Columbus, met with Union colonel Benjamin M. Prentiss, the commander in charge at Camp Defiance in Cairo, Illinois, on May 6, 1861, to reassure him that the militia forces in western Kentucky would not be used to fight against the forces at Cairo. In the meeting, Tilghman made this point clear when he stated, "We do not wish war. We are now electing our representatives to Congress, with the intention of holding out the olive branch. But the commerce of Kentucky is large, and our people do not understand how much of it is to be interrupted in transitu. They feel that they cannot ship a barrel of flour without being subjected to this system of espionage, which is entirely inadmissible." Tilghman felt the meeting was important so that he could alleviate any fears that the Union commander had to make sure that Kentucky's economic trade on the Ohio River was not disrupted by a Union blockade.[16]

While the Jackson Purchase would have seceded with the other Southern states, the rest of Kentucky did not agree with it, and on May 20, 1861, the Kentucky legislature voted to remain neutral. Albert P. Thompson, a prominent lawyer in Paducah, wrote a letter to the

Above: Lloyd Tilghman statue in Paducah. *Photo by author.*

Left: Brigadier General Benjamin M. Prentiss. *Library of Congress.*

Confederate secretary of war, Leroy Polk Walker, requesting aid to be sent to defend the Purchase area against the Union army stationed at Cairo. Thompson lamented that Kentucky chose neutrality, stating, "Our Legislature have so far disgraced themselves and to the extent of their power sullied the fair fame of Kentucky in not arousing our people and calling a convention." While requesting arms to fight against the Union army in case it invaded the Jackson Purchase, Thompson wrote, "Should Lincoln attempt to invade the South from Illinois, an intention of which is now evidenced by his concentration of a large body of troops at the mouth of the Ohio River, we, with arms in our hands, would resist to the death."[17]

With such a high level of discontent with the Kentucky legislature for remaining neutral, a convention met in Mayfield, Kentucky, on May 29 to discuss the possibility of the Jackson Purchase separating from Kentucky and uniting with Tennessee. Despite many fiery speeches against the Union and Kentucky neutrality, there was not enough of a consensus for leaving the state. But many of the same delegates at this convention met later in Russellville, Kentucky, to form a provisional Confederate government for the state.[18]

An event occurred in Columbus, Kentucky, on June 12, 1861, that put Kentucky's neutrality to the test. The Federal steamboat *City of Alton*, carrying two companies of the Eighth Illinois Infantry and accompanied by Colonel Oglesby, noticed, as they were passing Columbus, a Confederate flag flying in the town. When they returned back upstream, Oglesby called out to the townsfolk to haul the flag down, and when they refused, Oglesby had some troops wade ashore to haul down the flag themselves and return to the boat, angering the townsfolk of Columbus with their willful ignoring of Kentucky's neutrality.[19]

Honorable Richard J. Oglesby. *Library of Congress.*

The editor of the local *Columbus Crescent* newspaper, Len G. Faxon, wrote a withering response to the

Simon Boliver Buckner, CSA. *Library of Congress.*

Union raid on Columbus: "When the bow-legged wooden-shoed, sour craut stinking, Bologna sausage eating, hen roost robbing Dutch sons of—had accomplished the brilliant feat of taking down the Secession flag on the river bank, they were pointed to another flag of the same sort." Faxon continued by saying, "Would that its folds had contained 1000 asps to sting 1000 Dutchmen to eternity unshriven."[20]

After this event at Columbus, General Simon Bolivar Buckner, the commander of all the State Guard, sent Colonel Tilghman with six companies to Columbus on June 24, 1861, to preserve Kentucky's neutrality. But in the first week of July, Colonel Tilghman resigned and went back to Paducah to recruit soldiers for the Confederate army.[21]

Tilghman took many of the men under his command from Paducah to Camp Boone, across the southern border of Kentucky near Clarksville, Tennessee, around July 20, 1861. His group of men was organized as the Third Kentucky Infantry, with the following officers: Lloyd Tilghman, colonel; Albert P. Thompson, lieutenant colonel; Ben Anderson, major; Captain Alford Boyd, assistant quartermaster; Captain J.S. Byers, assistant commissary sergeant; Dr. J.W. Thompson, surgeon; and Dr. J.B. Sanders, assistant surgeon. The Third Confederate Infantry was organized into a brigade with the Second, Fourth and Ninth Kentucky and was put under the command of General Buckner, who resigned from the Kentucky State Guard shortly after Tilghman left.[22]

Kentucky's neutrality took another hit on August 10, 1861, when the *W.B. Terry*, an armed steamer that belonged to a group of Paducahians, captured a Louisville steamer called the *Pocahontas*, which was hauling tobacco at Pine Bluff, a town in Calloway County on the Tennessee River. Afterward, it delivered the steamer upstream to the Confederates. When the *W.B. Terry* returned to Paducah, the U.S. gunboat *Lexington* captured the steamer while it was in port on August 22, 1861, and took it back to Cairo, Illinois. But this action angered the captain and crew of the *Terry*, and the captain led a group of forty or fifty armed Paducah citizens to take control of the Paducah–Evansville mail packet called the *Samuel Orr* and move it up the Tennessee River in retaliation. The captain and crew of the *Samuel Orr* were able to escape using skiffs, and when the incident was reported to Colonel Richard Oglesby in Cairo, tensions grew to a boiling point between the Union army and the citizens of the Jackson Purchase, who were seen as being complicit with aiding the Confederate army.[23]

The citizens of Paducah were in an uproar, and just two days earlier, a small force of Union soldiers had crossed over the Ohio River and arrested three Ballard County men, reinforcing the town's fears that the Union troops in Cairo were going to invade soon. Quintus Quigley described the scene in the city: "Our city is now all excitement, a thousand puerile plans for retaliation by men who never had the coolness or judgment to plan the capture of a hen roost."[24]

Chapter 2

Kentucky Invaded

Prelude to Invasion

After Fort Sumter fell to the Confederacy, the State of Kentucky adamantly tried to remain neutral, and during this time, both Union and Confederate armies tried to place their forces on the most tactical points on Kentucky's borders, especially in the west, next to the Mississippi River. The Union army set up its headquarters at Cairo, Illinois, and Bird's Point, Missouri, at the confluence of the Ohio and Mississippi Rivers, and the Confederate army set up at Union City, Tennessee, and New Madrid, Missouri, just across the border from southwest Kentucky. Each side maintained readiness in case the opposing army made an incursion into Kentucky to gain the most desirable strategic locations within the Jackson Purchase, as each thought that losing this ground to the other would be detrimental to the war effort.

One such place desired by both the Union and Confederate armies was Columbus, Kentucky, due to its high bluffs overlooking the Mississippi River, creating a natural defensive position that would be able to control the opposing side's river vessels at that point. By putting artillery batteries on these bluffs, the side that controlled this area could effectively control the Mississippi River Valley for the Missouri, Kentucky and Tennessee areas, with fewer troops needed to defend.

If one were to ask the residents of Columbus, during this time, which side they preferred to occupy their city, they would have wholeheartedly approved of the Confederate army. In fact, residents of Columbus sent

Jefferson Davis. *Library of Congress.*

a letter to Confederate president Jefferson Davis on April 22, 1861, asking for a garrison of troops to protect them from the Union army. "We are all with you heart and hand—your friends to the death!," the letter exclaimed. "Columbus, too, is also a very important place, and should be garrisoned and fortified." The letter continued by stating that the "Mississippi here is very narrow, only half a mile wide, and to the north of the town are the iron banks—immense bluffs, which rise 200 feet above the river. An efficient battery planted there would effectually command the channel. Nothing could pass without our permission."[25]

In the last week of April, Union troops began setting up Camp Defiance in Cairo, Illinois, and Camp Smith, a short distance farther north. This position had an obvious strategic advantage in southeast Missouri and southern Illinois, as this point could control all the river traffic going south on the Mississippi River and would allow close scrutiny of western Kentucky. In the *Memphis Daily Appeal* on April 26, 1861, it was reported that one thousand Federal troops were in Cairo, Illinois, and that four thousand more would soon arrive. The paper supposed that the object of the Union deployment was to blockade the Mississippi River where the Ohio River joins it to prevent "all boats passing down which shall contain provisions or warlike stores."[26]

In May 1861, General Gideon Pillow was the commander of the Army of Tennessee, and he saw Columbus as the key to protecting Tennessee. Kentucky's neutrality was a problem for him, and on May 15, he sent a message to the Confederate secretary of war Leroy Polk Walker asking for support "in assuming a position on the new line near Union City or at Columbus. No answer yet...Must move without loss of time, else will be too late." Pillow told Walker that he sent a messenger to the governor of Kentucky, Beriah Magoffin, who was known to be sympathetic to the Southern cause, to ask him for permission to occupy and fortify Columbus;

Reaching out for the river: the drill grounds of the defenders of Cairo, Illinois. *Library of Congress.*

if he said no, he believed he should go "forward and occupy the work upon the ground of its necessity for protecting Tennessee." Pillow feared that the enemy would seize Columbus before he could get a large enough force together to occupy the city. Pillow also sent a letter to President Jefferson Davis on May 16, saying that he could occupy and fortify Columbus with "half the force required to defend the interior line, and as a necessity of my position I must occupy that position." However, on May 19, the Kentucky governor wrote a letter to President Davis asking assurance that the "Government of the Confederate States will continue to respect and observe the neutral position of Kentucky."[27]

Later, on July 12, 1861, President Davis appointed General Leonidas Polk to be the commander of the Confederate forces in Tennessee and upper Mississippi, also called Military Department Number Two, which comprised the lands west of the Tennessee River to the Mississippi River, with Missouri and Arkansas being added shortly afterward. After taking command, Polk then sent General Pillow to New Madrid, Missouri, to try to keep the Union forces from taking complete control of that state.[28]

With the buildup of Union forces in Cairo, and across the Mississippi River at Bird's Point, Missouri, General Polk began to receive concerned reports from citizens in western Kentucky. On July 30, D.O. Dixon, from Columbus, reported that the guns at Cairo were being removed to Bird's

General Leonidas Polk, CSA. *Library of Congress.*

Point and that there were seven thousand men at that place, with two thousand more expected to arrive. He also stated that two thousand men were with Union general Frémont in Cape Girardeau. In another report on August 3, by J.P. Gray from Columbus, eight steamboats with troops landed at Cairo on the second, and their pickets were as far down as Belmont, across the river from Columbus.[29]

In Blandville, Kentucky, on August 6, Charles Wickliffe wrote a letter to General Polk warning him of a possible invasion, stating, "We are threatened with invasion by General Prentiss, as he said to two of our citizens Saturday afternoon that after the August election 'Kentucky neutrality would go up,' and that he intended to send a military escort with Mr. Thomas Owens to Milburn to-day." He also said that "he should send reconnoitering parties into Kentucky to watch the enemy in Tennessee." He noted that he was "expecting orders to occupy Kentucky" and that when his troops came into Kentucky, the people should "change to Union men or keep their mouths shut…We shall try to defend ourselves against aggression upon our political and personal rights."[30]

On August 5, 1861, the Kentucky state elections for the legislature occurred. The Union Party won in the House of Representatives, seventy-six seats to twenty-four for the Southern Rights side. In the Senate, it won twenty-seven seats to eleven. This told General Polk and the other leaders in the Confederacy that Kentucky was pro-Union, even if the seven Jackson Purchase counties elected secessionist candidates without opposition. Because the Union candidates won most of the other regions in Kentucky by big margins, the results of the election showed that if the Confederates decided to invade Kentucky, it would be a very unpopular move with the pro-Union Kentucky legislature.[31]

On August 10, 1861, the *New York Times* mocked the *Paducah Herald*, which it called "a strong secession organ in that State," when editor John C. Noble wrote before the Kentucky elections, "Let us make the fight for the Legislature. Let it be done upon the fair issue of Secession or No Secession—to remain with the Abolition North or join the South—to remain a Slave State or abolish Slavery. Let us be honest. We all mean Secession. Magoffin means it. Breckinridge means it. Powell means it. Burnett means it. We all mean it. Then why not say so, and come out and advocate it openly and honestly?" The *Times* responded after the secessionists lost the Kentucky election in most of the areas except the Jackson Purchase by stating, "We hope the Herald is satisfied with the response of the people."[32]

General Gideon J Pillow, CSA. NARA—528290. *Wikimedia Commons.*

General Pillow was not impressed with the fortifications at New Madrid, Missouri, and he wrote to General Polk on August 28, saying, "My judgment therefore is, that the value of this position is greatly overrated." Pillow believed that Columbus was the key and that there was no time to waste, and in the letter, he said, "That time, I think, has arrived. Kentucky is now a boiling cauldron…Kentucky neutrality is no longer regarded, if indeed it

John Charles Frémont. *Library of Congress.*

ever was…If you do not intend to let the enemy take possession of that gateway [Columbus], you must take it first. If he gets possession of it once, you can never dislodge him. Its possession is a military necessity, involving the ultimate safety of Tennessee from devastating invasion."[33]

General Pillow believed that Kentucky neutrality was broken by the Union forces when it was discovered that Brigadier General William "Bull" Nelson had established Camp Dick Robinson in Garrard County, Kentucky. The soldiers there were recruited from men living within northeastern, central and central-southern Kentucky. On August 19, Governor Magoffin protested to President Lincoln, but he was told that the camp consisted exclusively of Kentuckians in the vicinity of their own homes. When Lincoln declined to remove the camp, many in the Confederacy believed that the neutrality of the state had been broken.[34]

Union major general John C. Frémont, who was assigned command of the Department of the West in May 1861, appointed Brigadier General Ulysses S. Grant on August 28 to take command of the forces in southeast Missouri and southern Illinois, and he was charged with the task of clearing the region of Confederate forces while headquartered at Cairo, Illinois. Occupying Columbus, Kentucky, was also seen as an important strategic step in gaining control of the Mississippi River Valley for the Federal forces, and Frémont wrote in his orders to Grant, "It is intended, in connection with all these movements, to occupy Columbus, Ky., as soon as possible."[35]

With this in mind, General Frémont sent Colonel Gustav Waagner to Belmont, Missouri, across the river from Columbus, Kentucky, on August 28 to "destroy the fortifications erecting by the rebels, keep possession of that place." He was told to use Belmont as a base and send troops to join up with forces moving toward Charleston, Missouri, to

Honorable B. Magoffin of Kentucky. *Library of Congress.*

help fight Confederate general Meriwether Jeff Thompson. However, when the Confederate forces witnessed Waagner's Union force moving into Belmont on the first and second of September, they believed that Columbus was going to be occupied by the Union forces. In Waagner's report to Frémont on the second, he stated, "At Columbus the rebels fly the secession flag from the top of a lofty pole in the center of the village in defiance of our gunboats. What shall I do with Columbus! What with Hickman! What with New Madrid!"[36]

After learning of the Union movement beginning to occupy Belmont, General Polk sent a letter to Kentucky governor Magoffin on September 1 to relay the understanding for his need to move his forces into the Jackson Purchase. Polk thought it was "of the greatest consequence to the Southern cause in Kentucky or elsewhere that I should be ahead of the enemy in occupying Columbus and Paducah." Paducah was not considered as important, given how it was not included in many of Polk's correspondences about the need to occupy Columbus. With this letter to Magoffin, however, he felt the need to add the city for strategic purposes, even though Paducah did not rank as high, to him, as Columbus.[37]

After General Grant arrived in Cairo, Illinois, he communicated to General Frémont on September 4 the possibility of taking the heights at Columbus: "On the strength of reconnaissances [*sic*] made by Colonel Waagner I telegraphed this evening that troops—artillery, cavalry, and infantry—can be spared from here by sending those from Jackson promptly to take possession of Columbus Heights, and New Madrid will fall within five days after. This should be done to-morrow night."[38]

THE WAR HAS ARRIVED IN KENTUCKY

On September 2, General Polk did not wait for a reply from Governor Magoffin when he ordered General Pillow to move into Kentucky, and on the third, they entered Hickman, Kentucky, unopposed. Pillow moved his forces by the Mississippi River from New Madrid to Hickman, and on the fourth, the main army marched overland and took control of the heights at Columbus. However, it was noticed by Union colonel Waagner at Belmont, and he reported that "on the night of Sept 2d and during this day the 3d there was an important movement of cavelry [*sic*] and infantry on the Heights in and near Columbus opposite this point but without any hostile demonstration."[39]

The Union army in Belmont left on the same day as Confederate forces were entering Columbus, and in a letter to President Davis on September 4, General Polk stated:

> *The enemy having descended the Mississippi River some three or four days since, and seated himself with cannon and intrenched* [sic] *lines*

> *opposite the town of Columbus, Ky., making such demonstrations as left no doubt upon the minds of any of their intention to seize and forcibly possess said town, I thought proper, under the plenary power delegated to me, to direct a sufficient portion of my command, both by river way and by land, to concentrated at Columbus, as well to* [afford] *to its citizens that protection they unite to a man in accepting, as also to prevent in time the occupation by the enemy of a point so necessary to the security of Western Tennessee. This demonstration on my part has had the desired effect. The enemy had withdrawn his force even before I had fortified my position.*[40]

On the same day that the main Confederate force entered Columbus, Commander John Rodgers on the U.S. gunboat *Tyler* sent a message to General Frémont near Cairo, Illinois, telling him about the events after he left Colonel Waagner at Belmont to make a reconnaissance down the river as far as Hickman. In the letter, he stated, "When we arrived in sight of Hickman we discovered a rebel gunboat, with the Confederate flag flying, off that town. The boat fired a shot at us, to which we replied; a number of tents extending for half a mile were upon the shore fronting the river. When three or four shots had been exchanged a battery on shore fired several guns, then another battery opened upon us." Commander Rodgers, after firing approximately twenty shots, decided to move away from Hickman back toward Cairo, and when they were passing Columbus, he stated, "Upon passing Columbus and the Chalk-Banks, we were fired upon by rebels with muskets. This was returned with muskets principally—but also by two great guns." Commander Rodgers concluded by noting that "the army at Hickman is considerable."[41]

Also, on September 4, General Grant, after communicating with Commander Rodgers, sent a message to General Frémont telling him about the withdrawal from Belmont: "On advice of Commander Rodgers I have ordered the withdrawal of troops from Belmont until such time as the column from Jackson may move."[42]

News of the Confederate's move into Kentucky was not received favorably by everyone in the South. Tennessee governor Isham G. Harris hastily sent a message to General Polk saying that he "just learned that Pillow's command is at Hickman. This is unfortunate, as the President and myself are pledged to respect the neutrality of Kentucky. I hope they will be withdrawn instantly, unless their presence there is an absolute necessity." On the same day, Secretary of War L.P. Walker went further by ordering

Portrait of Captain John Rodgers. *Library of Congress.*

a "prompt withdrawal from Kentucky," but when President Davis responded to General Polk, he only stated, "The necessity justifies the action."[43]

Senator Isham G. Harris from Tennessee. *Library of Congress.*

General Polk sent a testy response to Governor Harris: "General Pillow was directed by me, under the plenary powers delegated to me by the President and not since revoked to move from his late position at New Madrid to Columbus, Ky., and in consequence of the armed position of the enemy, who had posted himself with cannon and intrenchments [*sic*] opposite Columbus, the general was forced to land at Hickman to avoid his cannon." Polk concluded by saying, "I regret that a movement so entirely acceptable to the people of Kentucky, or at least this portion of Kentucky, and so essential to the security of Western Tennessee, does not permit me, in the exercise of the above authority, to concur with your views. I had never received official information that the President and yourself had determined upon any particular course in reference to the State of Kentucky."[44]

General Grant's Response to Columbus and Hickman

General Grant arrived at Cairo on September 4, and on the fifth, one of General Frémont's paid scouts, Charles A. de Arnaud, a Russian who had just arrived after traveling from Memphis and Union City, reported that Hickman and Columbus were occupied and that Confederate troops were sent out to take Paducah. In Arnaud's report to Frémont, he stated, "Just arrived from Memphis and Union City, Tenn. The enemy is marching in large force to take Paducah, on the Ohio River, to invade Southern Illinois. Our occupation of Paducah will frustrate the enemy's plans and secure for us the Tennessee River. Have communicated this to General Grant. He will move at once. No time to lose."[45]

When Grant left for Paducah, he left General John McClernand in command at Cairo, and McClernand sent a message to General Frément explaining the actions in and around Cairo on September 5: "This afternoon vigorous measures were adopted for an expedition for the seizure of the city of Paducah, 50 miles above, on the Ohio River. To prevent opposing measures, all passing on the rivers and roads was suspended, egress from the city forbidden, and the telegraph restrained."[46]

General Grant did not know if General Frémont received his own messages on September 5 because he did not receive any responses, and in Grant's memoirs, he wrote, "Not having received an answer to my first dispatch, I again telegraphed to department headquarters that I should start for Paducah that night unless I received further orders." Afterward, Grant sent a message explaining his action to Frémont about setting out from Cairo: "I left Cairo at 10:30 o'clock last night, taking two gunboats and three steamboats, with the Ninth Illinois, under Gen. E.A. Paine; the Twelfth Illinois, under Col. J. McArthur, and Smith's battery, four pieces light

U.S. Grant and staff. *Library of Congress.*

artillery, under Lieutenant Willard. I met with some detention at Mound city, owing to an accident to one of the steamers, creating a necessity for a transfer of troops. During the detention I was joined by Captain Foote, U.S. Navy, who accompanied the expedition."[47]

Actually, General Frémont did send a response, telling General Grant, "If you feel strong enough, you will take possession of Paducah; but if not, then opposite that place, on the Illinois side of the river, which you will do without delay, with the view of planting a battery which shall command the Ohio and the mouth of the Tennessee River. In a few days I will send an adequate force with sufficient artillery to hold that position. If in your power, it would be well to make preparation for building a bridge to connect the Illinois shore with Paducah." Grant, however, did not receive this message before he left because he wrote a message saying that he was heading for Paducah and to contact him if he should not go. There have been many questions as to why Grant did not receive the response from Frémont when the records show that one was sent on September 5. In the Papers of Ulysses S. Grant, it is mentioned that Frémont's message was written in Hungarian and possibly not translated for Grant before he left for Paducah, most likely due to the fact that Grant and his staff may have not known what to do with it.[48]

As General Grant was preparing to leave, he also sent a message to the Kentucky Speaker of the House that read, "I regret to inform you that Confederate forces in Considerable numbers have invaded the territory of Kentucky, and are occupying & fortifying strong positions at Hickman & Chalk Bluffs." He also issued special orders to all of the post commanders through Captain William S. Hillyer that noted:

> *The people of South-West Kentucky, having permitted large bodies of armed men in rebellion to the government, to assemble upon her soil, to erect Batteries and fire upon the Federal Flag, are guilty of an offence which must be resisted and punished. All commanders therefore, on the Kentucky borders, within this military District, are directed to embarass their communications with Rebels in every way possible. To this end all ferry's, yawls, flats and other boats within the reach of these troops, will be seized and taken in charge. Such orders as may be necessary for carrying into execution this order, will be promulgated at once by Post Commanders.*[49]

General Grant's fleet arrived at Paducah at 8:30 a.m. on September 6, and upon arriving, numerous secession flags were seen flying over the city, making it apparent that the citizens were anticipating the approach of

Paducah Riverfront showing the entrance to the Tennessee River. *Photo by author.*

the rebel army. Grant wrote that as he approached the city, Confederate Brigadier General Lloyd Tilghman and his staff left the city by the railroad, taking with them all the rolling stock. Grant was able to land his troops and take possession of the city without firing a gun.[50]

Colonel John McArthur's Twelfth Illinois regiment landed at the Marine Hospital, which was in the lower part of the city, and General Eleazer A. Paine's Ninth Illinois regiment landed at the foot of Broadway. The Twelfth Illinois took control of the hospital, and the Ninth Illinois marched up Broadway toward the Ohio and New Orleans railroad depot. It was noticed that before the soldiers disembarked, all of the secession flags had disappeared, and after landing, Grant had U.S. flags raised in their place.[51]

After taking control of the railroad depot, Grant stated that a large number of complete rations and almost two tons of leather were found, which he said was marked for the Confederate army. Also, the Union forces took control of the telegraph office to enable the ability to send telegraph dispatches in the future, and a number of letters and dispatched were seized. In the September 11 *St. Louis Democrat* newspaper, it was recorded that

Commander John Rogers "immediately took possession of the telegraph office. He was refused admittance, but the prompt application of the butts of muskets in the hands of his marines, gave quick entrance. It was found that the battery of the office had been carried off. The wires were immediately cut. The Post-office was next searched, and a large number of the most violent secession letters to rebels in the South were found."[52]

With the arrival of the Federal troops in the city, many of the citizens were completely taken by surprise. Grant stated that he "never after saw such consternation depicted on the faces of the people. Men, women and children came out of their doors looking pale and frightened at the presence of the invader. They were expecting rebel troops that day." Grant believed that nearly four thousand men from Columbus were within ten or fifteen miles from Paducah, and he stated, "I had but two regiments and one battery with me, but the enemy did not know this and returned to Columbus. I stationed my troops at the best points to guard the roads leading into the city." Grant continued, saying, "I addressed a short printed proclamation to the citizens of Paducah assuring them of our peaceful intentions, that we had come among them to protect them against the enemies of our country, and that all who chose could continue their usual avocations with assurance of the protection of the government. This was evidently a relief to them; but the majority would have much preferred the presence of the other army."[53] The proclamation read as follows:

PROCLAMATION,
TO THE CITIZENS OF
PADUCAH!

I have come among you, not as an enemy, but as your friend and fellow-citizen, not to injure or annoy you, but to respect the rights, and to defend and enforce the rights of all loyal citizens. An enemy, in rebellion against our common Government, has taken possession of, and planted its guns upon the soil of Kentucky and fired upon our flag. Hickman and Columbus are in his hands. He is moving upon your city. I am here to defend you against this enemy and to assert and maintain the authority and sovereignty of your Government and mine. I have nothing to do with opinions. I shall deal only with armed rebellion and its aiders and abetors. You can pursue your usual avocations without fear or hindrance. The strong arm of the Government is here to protect its friends, and to punish only its enemies. Whenever it is manifest that you are able to defend yourselves, to maintain

> *the authority of your Government and protect the rights of all its loyal citizens, I shall withdraw the forces under my command from your city.*[54]

General Grant left two gunboats and one of the steamboats at Paducah and placed the city under the command of General Eleazer A. Paine before leaving Paducah at noon. On the fifth, Grant ordered the Eighth Missouri Volunteers, commanded by Colonel Morgan L. Smith, which was stationed at Cape Girardeau, to report to Cairo immediately. It was to arrive in the evening in Paducah to reinforce Paine. In a message to General Frémont, Grant requested that two additional pieces of artillery to be added to Captain Smith's battery, commanded by Lieutenant Willard and also known as the Chicago Light Artillery, to help protect the city from any future attack.[55]

Before leaving Paducah, General Grant left instructions for General Paine:

> *Upon my departure you will assume command of the troops at this post, and make such disposal of the forces as will best enable you to retain possession and control of the city. A portion of the troops can be quartered at the Marine Hospital. You are charged to take special care and precaution that no harm is done to inoffensive citizens; that the soldiers shall not enter any private dwelling nor make any searches unless by your orders, and then a detail shall be made for that purpose. Exercise the strictest discipline against any soldier who shall insult citizens or engage in plundering private property. Make frequent reports to me at district headquarters, and also to the Department of the West, at Saint Louis, sending me copies of such reports.*[56]

When General Grant sent the message to the Kentucky Speaker of the House on September 5, it was not taken well by General Frémont, and Major Joseph H. Eaton was instructed to send a message to Grant on September 6 directing him that "Brigade and other Commanders are not to correspond with State or other high authorities, in matters pertaining to any branch of the public service, either in initiating such correspondence or in replying thereto. All such subjects are to be submitted to the Major General Commanding the Department for his information and action, by telegraph if of immediate importance, otherwise by regular course of mail."[57]

Also on September 6, General Frémont ordered Brigadier General Charles F. Smith, General Grant's former commandant at West Point, to travel to Paducah and take command in Paducah and all areas on the Kentucky side of the Mississippi and Ohio Rivers, to enable Grant to personally continue to command all of the forces at Cairo, Bird's Point, Cape Girardeau and Ironton. Frémont was adamant that Grant continue the building of Fort Holt, which was across from Cairo in Kentucky on the Mississippi River, because this triangle of forts at Cairo, Bird's Point and Fort Holt would completely control the river at that point.[58]

While in command at Paducah, General Paine ruled with an iron fist, which angered many of the residents in the city, and in a message that he sent to General Grant, this was highlighted when he said, "An accidental discharge of one of the 64s, on the Gun Boats gave the people an idea of a Gun Boat, and its efficiency…A Blacksmith refused to shoe a horse for me. I arrested him and gave him five minutes to shoe the Horse or be shot, he immediately went to work. I am compelled to be severe for nearly every man here is a rank secessionist." It is true that there were many secessionists in town, but from this message, it appeared that Paine did not follow Grant's instructions to not offend the citizens of Paducah.[59]

It was fortunate for the citizens of Paducah when General Smith arrived in the city on evening of the eighth to relieve General Paine, and while traveling to Paducah, he was directed to begin building defensive earthworks throughout the town. The main fort would later be known as Fort Anderson, and it was to be built around the Marine Hospital on Hospital Street. General Frémont informed General Grant to also make sure that Smith placed an artillery battery at the Marine Hospital and at Cross Creek and to prepare for forward movements to Mayfield as soon as reinforcements arrive.[60]

General Smith, writing to Frémont concerning the building of the earthworks, stated that he

> *rode around the town, and in advance of it yesterday, in company with Genl Paine and Col Webster (Engineer) and made a general disposition of the Troops. Col Webster is now out making, with a loyal person well acquainted with the vicinity, a reconnoissance* [sic] *and plan for the commencement of the works. I will enclose before finishing this a sketch of the roads and position of the troops. A bridge to Brooklyn* [today's Brookport] *of boats or other material, however desirable, will be exceedingly difficult of accomplishment, if at all, in any reasonable time. Brooklyn is some three miles below this. The river is from 3/5 to 3/4 of a mile wide.*

General Frémont also directed General Grant to have Smith begin making plans to occupy Smithland with four companies as soon as they could be spared because the Cumberland River met the Ohio River at this point,

Right: General Charles F. Smith. *Library of Congress.*

Below: Fort Anderson, Paducah, Kentucky. *Library of Congress.*

which was an important strategic point desired by both sides in the war because of the ability to move troops southward using this river, as well as the Tennessee River, deep into the Confederacy.[61]

The citizens of Paducah were in a state of fear, shock and anger when the Union troops entered the city and began occupying different locations for their use. The occupation of Paducah was reported differently in the newspapers, depending on which side the reporter favored in the war, but it was clear in many of the accounts that the citizens were very unhappy with the arrival of General Grant's forces. In the *St. Louis Democrat*, the mood of the city was described:

> *A sullen, gloomy aspect pervaded the city, indicative of the most rebellious and obstinate feeling. Every place of business was closed. Knots of men stood at every corner, with knit, compressed brows and quivering lips, and occasionally a suppressed cheer would arise for Jeff. Davis, and curses on what they termed Lincoln's abolition troops. The troops, with heavy, measured tread, marched on. As we got further up town women and children ran out and cheered for Jeff. Davis. The women seemed crazed with excitement...On Friday and Saturday Main street was perfectly choked with carriages and vehicles, containing families and household furniture, leaving the city for points back in the country. Many went over to Illinois. A perfect panic seemed to possess them, which no assurance of our officers or troops could allay. They had got the idea into their heads that Pillow was advancing on us, that in case of an attack the town would be shelled and burned by our gunboats.*[62]

The *St. Louis Republican* described the residents of Paducah:

> *Here in Paducah considerable terror has arisen among the inhabitants, and thousands would leave if they could. Household furniture is being removed in skiffs, and what other conveyances can be got, to safer points. If affairs in Kentucky continue in their present state three weeks longer, the town will be almost depopulated. Although numberless elegant residences are deserted and stand silent monuments of blighting secession, society seems to have already fled, and gloom and horror take possession. Not a carriage is seen upon the streets, or lady upon the beautiful walks.*

The article continued describing the residents still in town, as well as their actions:

> *In no place yet have I seen so bitterly hostile a feeling existing against the Union as here. Scowling, angry glances watch with what seems an intense hatred, every movement of a passing soldier. Some of the wells have been poisoned where the camps get their water, and many similar acts perpetrated. Secession is the rule, and Union the rare exception. Whether Uncle Sam has any medicine as strong as the complaint, is still an open question. On the streets people wear secession caps, and boast that before the week closes every Federal will be driven out.*[63]

The *Louisville Courier* carried an account from the Cairo correspondent of the *Cincinnati Enquirer* that noted:

> *The proclamation that the Lincoln troops went there to protect the citizens, it will be seen was not appreciated. They are looked upon as invaders… The citizens did not appear to appreciate the favor. They closed all their houses of business, and most of the male citizens left town for the present. Some of the women jeered the troops on their passage through the town, calling them "Abolition invaders," &c., and repeatedly cheering for Jeff. Davis and the Confederate States.*[64]

Showing that Paducah had made a favorable impression on some of the Federal soldiers, a Union soldier with the Eighth Illinois Infantry, Charles W. Wills, wrote about his time while in Paducah: "I fell in love with Paducah while I was there, and I think I will settle there when the war is over. I never saw so many pretty women in my life. All fat, smooth-skinned small boned, highbred looking women. They hollered 'Hurrah for Jeff' at us, some of them, but that's all right. I could write until to-morrow morning about Paducah, but I must go and confiscate some corn for dinner."[65]

On September 22, the *New York Times* printed an account of the building of the pontoon bridge that General Frémont had ordered General Smith to build across the Ohio River to the Illinois shore:

> *Heavy guns are being brought up from Cairo, breastworks thrown up, munitions of war daily arriving, and the place hourly growing stronger. While I write, a dozen steamboats, pouring from their chimneys immense volumes of dense black smoke, and laboriously puffing forth their white, hard-drawn breath, are busily engaged in towing barges to and fro, to form a bridge across the Ohio at this point. When completed, it will be an immense affair, capable of sustaining a whole Army at a single burden. It*

> *is evident, from the building of this bridge, that our Generals appreciate the vital importance of Paducah, and that it will figure, largely in the history of the expedition of the Mississippi.*

The *New York Times* described the bridge the next day: "They are laid side by side, and a platform, giving much the appearance of a plank-road, passes over the middle. In a few days the Ohio here will be crossed by a highway, which, while affording passage for any number of soldiers and the heaviest artillery, can be moved at pleasure, or, as the exigencies of the day require, to points above or below." However, the pontoon bridge was not to be a long-term structure, as on October 8, the bridge was carried away when the river rose suddenly by twelve or fifteen feet.[66]

Regarding the pontoon bridge, on October 2, Aaron Loder Mastin, a soldier with the Forty-first Illinois Volunteer Infantry, gave an account of the bridge in his diary: "As I have not said anything to you about the floating bridge, here's how I will give a description of it. It is composed of flat boats run up side by side and sleepers or ties thrown across them and then planked over that again so I think when high water comes it will all wash away." His assumption of the bridge being washed away ended up being correct.[67]

After the occupation of Paducah, General Grant felt fortunate, as General Prentiss (in command at Cairo) turned himself in at St. Louis to be arrested because he was angered that Grant was given command over him. When this caused the stoppage of the Union expedition against General Thompson in Missouri, Grant later said that it "proved very fortunate that the expedition against Jeff. Thompson had been broken up. Had it not been, the enemy would have seized Paducah and fortified it, to our very great annoyance."[68]

OUTCOME OF THE INVASIONS IN KENTUCKY

Even though Kentucky governor Beriah Magoffin was sympathetic to the South, the Kentucky legislative elections on August 5 helped determine how the state would react to the invasion of Kentucky. Because the Union candidates won by large margins, giving them control in the legislature, any move that the Confederates made in Kentucky was sure to be seen unfavorably, regardless of the secessionist candidates winning their seats in the Jackson Purchase.

On September 9, John M. Johnson, chairman of committee from the Kentucky Senate, sent General Polk a copy of its resolution that was adopted

Major Robert Anderson. *Library of Congress.*

after being given the intelligence of the "military occupation of Hickman, Chalk Bank, and Columbus." He stated, "I need not say that the people of Kentucky are profoundly astonished that such an act should have been committed by the Confederate States, and especially that they should have been the first to do so with an equipped and regularly organized army." Johnson continued, "In obedience to the thrice repeated will of the people, as expressed at the polls and in their name, I ask you to withdraw your forces from the soil of Kentucky." Polk responded by telling Johnson that he would agree to "withdraw the Confederate troops from Kentucky, provided she will agree that the troops of the Federal Government be withdrawn simultaneously, with the guarantee (which I will give reciprocally for the Confederate Government) that the Federal troops shall not be allowed to enter nor occupy any part of Kentucky for the future."[69]

The Kentucky legislature, in response to the invasion of the Confederate armies in Kentucky, overrode the veto of Governor Magoffin and passed legislation to require him to issue a proclamation, on September 18, requiring the Confederate forces to be expelled from the state of Kentucky because "the commanders of the forces so invading the State have insolently prescribed the conditions upon which they will withdraw, thus insulting the dignity of the State by demanding terms to which Kentucky cannot listen without dishonor." The proclamation further required the assembling of Kentucky national troops, with General Robert Anderson, a native Kentuckian, who was appointed "to the command of the Department of Cumberland, be requested to take instant command, with authority and power from this Commonwealth to call out a volunteer force in Kentucky for the purpose of repelling the invaders from our soil."[70]

Those opposed to the fact that only the Confederacy was being forced to leave Kentucky (especially the Jackson Purchase House and Senate members) did try to add to the law a resolution that requested the governor demand the immediate withdrawal of both the Federal and Confederate troops from the southwestern part of the state, but it was defeated by a vote of twenty-nine to sixty-eight. The unionists in the legislature won their resolution to expel just the Confederates by a vote of seventy-one to twenty-six in the House, as well as twenty-five to eight in the Senate.[71]

Chapter 3
Early Occupation

Building the Defenses

When General Grant's Federal forces first occupied Paducah, they began immediately preparing defenses around and within the town to thwart a Confederate attack that they believed was eminent. One of Brigadier General Charles F. Smith's first tasks when he arrived in Paducah on September 8 to take over from Brigadier General Eleazer Paine was to begin building the defenses around the city and also start the construction of Fort Anderson around the Marine Hospital. Smith was a career military man who was commandant of cadets at West Point; General Grant and General Sherman were cadets under him before the war. In one account, John H. Page, a soldier in Battery A of the Chicago Light Artillery, described Smith, "To me he was the handsomest man I had ever seen. His long white mustache, erect figure, soldiery appearance and dignity combined, left an ineffaceable imprint on my memory."[72]

The fortification of Paducah was described in a few articles in the *New York Times*, and in one article that was a reprint from an article in the *St. Louis Democrat* on October 16, 1861, it described the outer defenses: "The town is now surrounded by formidable defences, garrisoned by an effective and powerful force (about 7,000 strong) and ready for an assault. The defences consist of six forts or earthworks, on which are mounted cannon of heavy calibre, the whole forming a half circle around the outskirts of the city." The building of Fort Anderson was also described: "One of the most important

Armies in western Kentucky. *Photo by author.*

of the preparations now going on, is that of fortifying the Marine Hospital. Immense earthworks are already completed partly around it, and will soon be finished entirely. Should an emergency occur, troops could retreat to this place and hurl defiance until starved out."[73]

The *New York Times* reprinted another article from the *Detroit Advertiser* that described the outer defenses: "When we came here the town was skirted by a dense forest of mostly young trees, but now for several hundred yards outside the batteries this timber is cut down, the branches chopped off about eighteen inches or two feet from the trunks of the trees, in such a manner as to leave the ends sharp, with the buts of the trees turned inward, and the limbs that will make stakes are sharpened and driven into the ground, thus making an obstruction that cannot be passed by either infantry or artillery." Later, on January 1, 1862, the *New York Times* described Fort Anderson further: "Anticipating an attack by the rebels from the direction of the Tennessee River, a strong fort has been erected, and now is nearly completed. It is called Fort Anderson in honor, I suppose, of the hero of Sumter and is situated on the bank of the Ohio, about a mile below the Tennessee. It surrounds a handsome building, now used as a marine hospital, and is mounted with guns, sufficient in quantity and weight to sink in twenty minutes all the rebel gunboats this side of the Gulf."[74]

Troubles Begin for General Smith

After General Smith took command of Paducah from General Paine, there could not have been more different styles of command. Whereas Paine ignored General Grant's orders for treating the citizens of Paducah with respect and patience, as well as threatening to shoot residents for not doing as he wished, Smith, who graduated from West Point and stayed in the army, was an old-line officer and professional soldier who followed his superiors' orders to the letter; his extensive knowledge of army matters highlighted the difference between volunteer soldiers like Paine and the regular army soldiers like Smith. Paine, also a West Point graduate, who had quit his commission many years before, began the war as the colonel of the Ninth Illinois Volunteers, and he was made a general on September 3 in Cairo, Illinois. Instead of rising through the ranks to achieve his rank from experience, as Smith did, Paine was an example of someone given their commission at the beginning of the war. This lack of trust in the volunteer officers and their untrained troops can be seen in a letter sent by Major General Henry W. Halleck to Major General George McClellan on December 6, 1861, complaining that he was "almost destitute of regular officers"; he believed that the volunteers were, with a few exceptions, entirely ignorant on how to perform their duties.[75]

John P. Hawkins—who, at the time, was the inspector commissary on Major General Halleck's staff—described General Smith as a "beau ideal soldier, in presence and in character, and skillful in the administration of military business. He at once organized everything at Paducah on a strictly military basis, and enforced the observance of regulation details. This made him unpopular with some of his command, and soon complaints were made by interested correspondents of newspapers, charging him with arbitrary conduct in his administration, and efforts were made through political machinery to have him relieved from his command, accusing him of all sorts of abuses, personal and official." The name given him by the correspondents by way of belittling was "Paducah Smith." Hawkins concluded that the command in Paducah was the best organized in all areas and was the "most

Major General Henry W. Halleck. *Library of Congress.*

soldierly and the best disciplined of any in the Division." However, many of the troops and officers felt that Smith was too lenient on the rebel sympathizers, and whereas Paine was too harsh, some of his men, and many of the newspapers, felt that Smith's loyalty to the Union should be questioned because he allowed them to openly speak about their secessionist views without repercussions.[76]

General Grant told other officers that he felt odd giving orders to General Smith, and he said as much when visiting Lieutenant Colonel Augustus L. Chetlain in Smithland, Kentucky: "I am going to Paducah to-night and will have to give Gen. Smith orders to-morrow morning, which don't seem just right to me, for this veteran officer was the commandant of West Point when I was a cadet and all the school regarded him as one of the very ablest officers of his age in the army." Grant was another who rose to the rank of general because of his connections; he was friends with Congressman Elihu B. Washburne from Galena, Illinois, and a political ally of President Abraham Lincoln. Grant was probably considered an unknown with those in the regular army because he was appointed colonel of the Twenty-first Illinois Volunteers by Illinois governor Richard Yates at the beginning of the war, even though he was West Point trained. This may be the reason why Smith was given Paducah after Grant occupied the city, and Grant probably did not help his case when he sent a message, before leaving for Paducah, to the Kentucky legislature informing its members of the reason why he was occupying Paducah before he left, upsetting his superiors for his acting without orders.[77]

General Smith wanted to send out reassurances to the citizens of Paducah, just as General Grant did when he issued his proclamation on September 6, and on October 10, he issued a statement to the citizens with the purpose to "show the inhabitants of this region that it was not the intention of the Government to interfere with their comfort and well being in any respect,

General U.S. Grant. *Library of Congress.*

not excepting those who were well known to sympathize with the people of the States in rebellion. The person and property of every one has been protected, and quiet and good order preserved. If any discomfort or annoyance has occurred, it has been incidental to a state of war and from military necessity." However, due to some bad behavior from some Paducah citizens, he was convinced that "the conciliatory policy ceases to be a virtue," which caused Smith to forbid "the outposts to pass out any person without a written permission from these headquarters, which will only be given to persons of approved loyalty to the Government of the United States. Nor will goods or stores of any description be permitted to pass out without the same permission."[78]

At the end of October, General Grant and his staff visited Paducah, and Grant and his adjutant general, Major John Rawlins, were assigned to stay in the house occupied by General Lew Wallace, later known for his writing the classic book *Ben-Hur*. That evening, Generals Smith, Grant and Wallace spent their time telling stories about the Mexican-American War while smoking cigars and drinking late into the evening and early morning; afterward, the evening was reported in the newspapers, as Wallace later wrote in his autobiography:

> *The week was hardly out before newspapers began reaching Paducah laden with lurid accounts of the meeting at my house. It was an orgie, a beastly drunken revel led by both Grant and Smith—so the story ran. There were liquors and cigars on the night in question, and some singing, but no intoxication or anything like a revel. Nevertheless, a charge against General Grant of habitual drunkenness arose about that time, and spread through the country, greatly to his mortification and detriment, and some of his friends, thinking the slander had its origin the night he was my guest*

in Paducah, were disposed to hold me responsible for the publicity of the affair. In self-defence, I finally traced the offensive articles to a regimental chaplain, and induced him to resign.[79]

PADUCAH AND THE BATTLE OF BELMONT

The Battle of Belmont occurred on November 7, 1861. General Smith had been ordered, on the first, to begin preparing to send out two different forces as a demonstration to the Confederates only and not to attack unless attacked from a similar-sized force—one to go to Melvin, Kentucky, twenty-five miles out from Paducah, and the other to go south to Viola, north of Mayfield, Kentucky. Both were ordered to have everyone carry three days' rations, march three days and then return back to Paducah; the first force was ordered to return via the Lovelaceville and Blandville Road, while the latter, which headed to Viola, was to return via the Melvin Road. Smith decided to send General Paine's First Brigade to march to Melvin, and the Second Brigade, under Colonel W.L. Sanderson, was chosen to march to Viola—both leaving a small force to guard the camps in Paducah. The purpose of these movements was to try to fool the Confederates at Columbus into thinking that they were being attacked from both sides of the Mississippi River, and the movement of Paine's force was to keep the Confederates from sending reinforcements across the river to attack General Grant. The intention of Sanderson's brigade was to watch and prevent the forces south of Mayfield in Camp Beauregard from attacking Paine's left flank or from behind.[80]

The next day, Paine, upon hearing the sounds of cannon fire coming from Columbus, went against Smith's orders and marched his force farther south to Milburn, Kentucky. Smith believed that Paine moved to the attack of Columbus with a "fixed purpose from the start to attempt to gain notoriety without reference to the public interests or his plain duty as a soldier." By moving farther southwest to Milburn, Paine was adding an extra day's march to the planned three-day march, and considering that the troops were raw recruits, this march was strenuous and exhausting. This extra day with no food also left them hungry, creating problems of stragglers that caused havoc to the local residents, and on the march back to Paducah, the men of the Fortieth and Forty-first Illinois Volunteers began throwing their overcoats, blankets and cooking gear to the ground to lighten their load, as well as

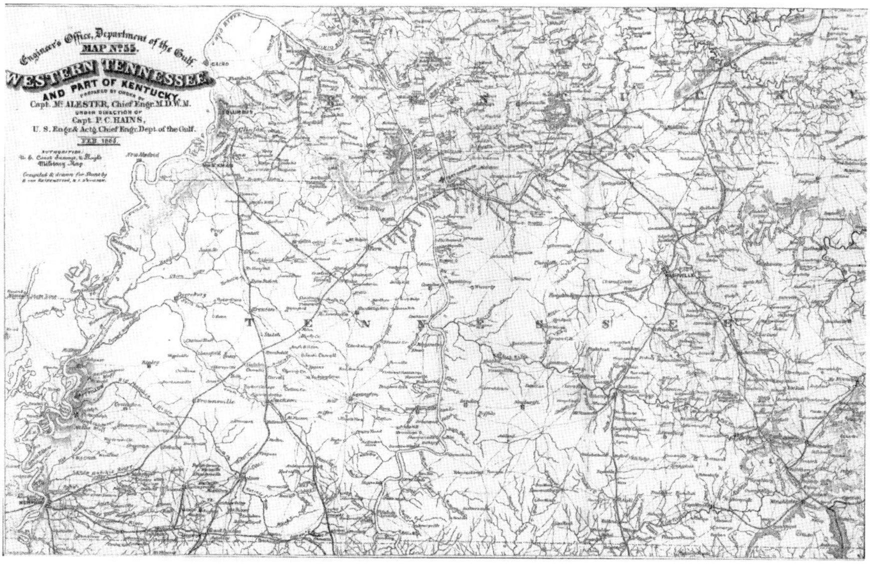

Map of western Kentucky and Tennessee, 1865. *Library of Congress.*

abandoning mules and army wagons. Smith was outraged seeing the ragged troops stumble into Paducah, some a day late, and on November 11, he issued General Orders No. 32, to be read at the head of every company in the camp.[81] It read as follows:[82]

> *Reports of the most painful character have reached the commanding general from different sources in regard to the conduct of a portion of Brig. Gen. E.A. Paine. The imputations are of the most discreditable, most disgraceful character to them as soldiers or citizens—that in returning, several regiments (the Ninth and Twelfth Illinois excepted) straggled home in parties without the semblance of military array—a mere armed mob; and that the property of citizens was wantonly destroyed, and in some instances robbery by violence committed. Such conduct implies a want of discipline that he can scarcely credit, and he calls upon the brigade and other commanders to use their utmost endeavors to remedy such a state of things. That unmerited censure may not attach to any one, the commanding general intends to ask for a legal investigation into conduct of all concerned.*

THE CONFEDERATE FLAG AT THE TILGHMAN HOUSE

On November 25, 1861, a group of Confederate officers under a flag of truce received permission from General Smith to enter Paducah. Afterward, they met at the Tilghman House on the corner of Court and Poplar Streets, located today at 631 Kentucky Avenue. The house was actually owned by Robert Owen Woolfolk, and before the war, General Lloyd Tilghman was given the use of the house for his family when he came to Paducah to help build a railroad to the city. But when he and his family left for him to join the Confederate army, the Woolfolk family moved back into the house. While they were meeting, General Lew Wallace decided to drill his Eleventh Indiana Infantry outside the Woolfolk home, and in response, Woolfolk, who was openly secessionist, raised a window and hung a Confederate flag out of it while shouting, "Hurrah for Jeff Davis!" This was not the first time this man and members of his family openly hung the Confederate flag, and each time, Smith allowed them to continue, angering the Union soldiers each time it happened.[83]

Wallace sent an aide up to the door to request that the flag be removed and was refused by Woolfolk, and in response, the aide called on a few soldiers of the Eleventh Indiana to remove the flag. When the soldiers returned with the flag, they tore it apart and threw it at the feet of the Confederate officers. When Wallace's aide tried to raise a U.S. flag in its place, he was knocked down by Woolfolk, which caused both the Union soldiers and Confederate officers to react by attacking one another in what became a brawl inside the home, making such a noise that it was heard outside. At this point, seeing that the situation was getting out of hand, Wallace sent for Smith, and he came quickly to the home and entered the house to break up the fight. As soon as Smith entered the house, the fighting ended, and a furious Smith apologized to the Woolfolk family and the Confederate officers, who were under a flag of truce; the soldiers who were involved in the fight were put under arrest and told to return to their quarters.[84]

After Wallace returned from speaking with Smith, Private John B. Day, a member of Battery A of the Chicago Light Artillery, remembered later in the *Paducah Sun* on February 23, 1905, "I can plainly see Gen. Wallace as he came walking from Gen. Smith's headquarters and mounting the fence beside the house and hear his tone of utter contempt as he said, 'You have had your will, get back to your camps.' The mob quickly and quietly disappeared."[85]

The Tilghman House is still located in Paducah at 631 Kentucky Avenue. It is now called the Lloyd Tilghman House and Civil War Museum. *Photo by author.*

In another account of the incident, while soldiers of the Eleventh Indiana were passing by the Woolfolk house, Woolfolk raised the Confederate flag and hurrahed for Jefferson Davis, which he had done on several occasions. As a result, Wallace was told of the "traitorous flag" flying across from the U.S. headquarters. Wallace sent his aide-de-camp, Captain Frederick Knefler, with a squad of men to the house with a U.S. flag to ask to have the offending flag taken down and, if he refused, to replace the Confederate flag with the Stars and Stripes. When Woolfolk refused, Wallace's aide forcibly took down the Confederate flag, called the Stars and Bars in the Confederacy, and hoisted the U.S. flag. When Woolfolk complained to Smith, he sent his aide, Lieutenant J.T. Price, to go and order Wallace to have the U.S. flag taken down, but Wallace refused, saying, "The flag should not be taken down while there was a live man in his brigade. When Knefler suggested that Woolfolk should sleep under a 'loyal flag' for one night, Price replied that he 'did not consider that any great honor.'" After hearing this, Knefler punched and knocked down Price, and Wallace had to break up the fight when cries of "kill him" were shouted out by several members of the Eleventh Indiana while some kicked at the helpless Price on the ground. It was said in another account that Wallace went with his old regiment to remove the flag in a procession headed by the bearer of the flag, and they were followed by their band playing "La Marseillaise." They played "The Star-Spangled Banner" when the U.S. flag was raised and then "Yankee Doodle." Afterward, they dispersed back to their camps.[86]

Because of General Smith's taking the side of Woolfolk, many in the Eleventh Indiana were angry with his actions that day, and some men from the Eighth Missouri Volunteers, another regiment in the brigade, were said to have commandeered a municipal fire engine and were on their way to flood his headquarters, but Wallace stopped them before they could do the deed.[87]

General Smith was furious with Wallace and all who participated. The next day, he issued General Orders No. 36, which stated that he was "compelled to denounce the transaction as a great violation of good order and military discipline; but he is inclined to the belief that those engaged in it will, upon reflection, come to regard it in that light themselves." He went on to say that "[a]lthough Kentucky is full of traitors, her Legislature left her one of the States of the Union; and our forces on her soil are charged with the high mission of protecting her people and sovereignty. More plainly, he desires every soldier, without regard to his position, to know that he is sent here by the Government as the protector of a loyal State, which, though occupied by rebel armies, is not an enemy's country; and that success requires him, by the patient exercise of moderation, obedience, and charity, to earn that character from both friends and foes."[88]

General Lew Wallace. *Library of Congress.*

Afterward, Lew Wallace regretted the incident, and he said later in his autobiography, "This affair, apparently so trifling, worked me an injury of long standing. Unfortunately, it furnished the newspapers a welcome theme. Accrediting me with the outbreak, they complimented my patriotism and denounced General Smith." Wallace continued, "From Paducah the story

Unidentified soldier of the Eleventh Indiana Infantry Regiment in Zouave uniform. *Library of Congress*.

passed to headquarters at Cairo, thence to headquarters at St. Louis, in both of which the military offense was seen and discussed as of my incitement."[89]

The newspapers did indeed pick up the story, and General Smith's patriotism was put to the test. A correspondent of the *Missouri Democrat* stated, "On Tuesday last a secessionist in Paducah by the name of Woolfolk, hung a secession flag out of his window as some of our troops were passing by, and hurrahed for Jeff. Davis. This man had done the same thing before, on several occasions, and the matter was reported to General Smith, but he refused to interfere. This refusal of Gen. Smith caused great indignation among the troops, and doubts of his loyalty were freely expressed in Paducah."[90]

General George B. McClellan. *Library of Congress.*

In the *Cincinnati Commercial*, the correspondent stated it clearly: "We all hope that the War Department may soon find a field of operation where the General in command may have an opportunity to display his loyalty more conspicuously than he has here." The *Chicago Tribune*, on December 11, stated, "What is the consequence, but that a disgust and a distrust of their commander pervades his entire force? It comes to us from every source. Our Cincinnati and St. Louis exchanges are full of it, and the omens are teeming and abundant that the Union cause cannot prosper in Kentucky with such leaders. When is there to be a change? Is this a war? Are we to have a war policy? Can it be carried on until such officers as Paducah Smith find their proper places in retirement, or in Secessia?"[91]

Fortunately for Smith, his superior, General Halleck, was also an old regular army soldier, and he had his back when he sent a message to General McClellan informing him of the situation and insisting that Smith was loyal. He told McClellan that Smith was needed where he was in Paducah. Smith told Wallace, after the incident and the newspaper attacks, that he knew who had been giving information to the media. He believed it to be General Paine of the Ninth Illinois.[92]

On December 23, General Paine was transferred from Paducah to command at Bird's Point, Missouri.[93]

CITY ESCAPES DESTRUCTION

All in all, Paducah was very fortunate to have escaped a deadly and destructive outcome while the city was on the front lines of the war. As the troops and gunboats went south to capture Fort Henry and Fort Donelson, the Confederate armies in Hickman, Columbus and Bowling Green were forced to move south to keep from getting flanked and surrounded by Grant's army. Paducah was now behind the Union lines in the war, and the secessionists in the city and in the Jackson Purchase were horrified when they learned that the Southern armies, including many of their sons, were moving away and leaving them in the hands of the Federal army. It was unknown to them if the Confederate armies would be able to win their way back.

In Paducah, General Smith understood that keeping the peace required his troops showing patience and respect to the pro-Confederate citizens to gain their peaceful cooperation, and after Smith left with the Union army, the citizens of Paducah had no way of knowing if the next commander would be like General Eleazer Paine or one like General Charles Smith. They hoped for the latter.

Chapter 4

Cesar Kaskel and General Grant's General Orders No. 11

This is the story of how the actions of Cesar Kaskel, a resident of Paducah during the Civil War, led to the ending of a Union military injustice that became known as the worst official anti-Semitic action in American history, when Major General Ulysses S. Grant issued General Orders No. 11 on December 17, 1862, instructing his officers to expel all the Jews in the military district of western Kentucky, western Tennessee and Mississippi:[94]

> *General Orders, Hdqrs, 13th A.C., Dept of the Tenn.,*
> *No. 11 Holly Springs, December 17, 1862.*
>
> *The Jews, as a class, violating every regulation of trade established by the Treasury Department, and also Department orders, are hereby expelled from the Department.*
>
> *Within twenty-four hours from the receipt of this order by Post Commanders, they will see that all of this class of people are furnished with passes and are required to leave, and any one returning after such notification will be arrested and held in confinement until an opportunity occurs of sending them out as prisoners.*
>
> *No permits will be given these people to visit Headquarters for the purpose of making personal application for trade permits.*
>
> *By order of Maj. Gen U.S. Grant:*
> *Jno. A. Rawlins,*
> *Assistant Adjutant-General.*

General Grant believed that Jewish traders were orchestrating an illegal trade of Southern cotton in his military district and delivering intelligence, gold and supplies to the enemy, but the order blamed the Jews as a class instead of singling out the individual traders. Since western Kentucky, western Tennessee and Mississippi were in Grant's military district, Grant was in charge of bestowing trading permits, and cotton was a lucrative trade, so he was being inundated with requests. He knew of the reports of goods being smuggled to the Confederacy, and he wanted to stop this practice.

The Civil War brought out the worst in some people. Mistrust and animosities grew steadily in the Four Rivers region due to the political differences, economic hardships and constant guerrilla attacks on residents that became a part of life in the area, and because of this, old-world prejudices and stereotypes soon occurred, singling out the Jewish residents in particular.

Because of the river systems located so close to Paducah and the railroad lines that went through the city, its growth, before the Civil War, grew steadily, and because of the river traffic, it was a good location to start businesses for many German immigrants, among them many of Jewish ancestry. Cesar Kaskel was born in the town of Rawitsch, Prussia, and during the 1850s, many German Jews left for the United States to escape from a world where there were legal limitations on where they could live and the kinds of jobs that they could do to make a living. Prussia, during this time, was going through domestic unrest due to a bad economy that created hardships for finding work, and Kaskel hoped to change all of that when he moved to Paducah, Kentucky, in 1858.[95]

Kaskel soon partnered with Solomon Greenbaum and went into business, but unfortunately, the Civil War began in 1861. Kaskel found that running a business during this time was a difficult task. On June 12, 1861, Southern trade was restricted by the Federal government to economically deprive the Confederates' ability to trade for war supplies. On September 6, 1862, General Grant landed troops at the riverfront in Paducah, causing even further economic hardships for Kaskel. Permits from the Union army were required before anyone was allowed to conduct business transactions after western Kentucky was declared to be under "insurrectionary influence," which allowed the Treasury Department to control the trading in the region to limit the ability for illegal trade to occur with the Confederacy.[96]

With all of the shortages in goods during the war and the Union army in control of Paducah, the speculators and smugglers fared very well, despite the attempts of the Federal government to halt illegal trade. Also, with the supply and demand problems created by the war, many unscrupulous deals were done to line many a pocket, giving some, with the right connections, more Federal trade permits, which gave them the ability to create a vast amount of wealth from the imbalance in trade.[97]

In small cities like Paducah, many residents were aware of these deals, and this created accusations of public corruption and personal animosities, either because they were blacklisted from getting permits because they were openly secessionist and branded as treasonous to the Union cause or because they were recent immigrants who had distinct European accents and different ways. The old-world stereotype of the Jewish immigrants came to the forefront, and many were denied permits because they were considered untrustworthy and unscrupulous in business. The unionists believed they were in league with the secessionists, smuggling goods to the Confederates, and the secessionists didn't trust the Paducah Jewish merchants because many openly supported the Union cause; in fact, Cesar Kaskel was the vice-president of the Paducah Union League Club, and his brother, Julius, was a recruiter for the Union army.[98]

To highlight how some in the Union army believed that the Jews were all smugglers, a report was wired from Union navy lieutenant S.L. Phelps to Flag Officer Andrew H. Foote on December 30, 1861, in which he complained that too much smuggling was occurring from Paducah to Evansville and that it was being done by "as usual chiefly by Jews."[99]

THE PROBLEMS WITH COTTON

When the war began, President Abraham Lincoln had a problem, and it was cotton; the South had it and everyone needed it. Both the European industries and the Northern industries in the United States needed the raw material and the Union army needed it for tents, but it was decided early on in the war to allow trade from the Border States to occur in the Confederate States so that permits would be given to private citizens that allowed cotton to be bought and brought north. This satisfied the Northern industrial interests that were continually requesting that the cotton trade be allowed to continue.[100]

The problem that General Grant had was when his armies marched south into Tennessee and Mississippi in 1862, where cotton was one of the main cash crops. He quickly learned how warfare had caused the

Abraham Lincoln. *Library of Congress.*

price of cotton to skyrocket to three or four times the prewar value, causing many to follow the army in the occupied towns to seek ways of acquiring cheap cotton from the South and to sell in the Northern states for a huge profit. Needless to say, some of the speculators following the army were not afraid to do many things to make a profit, including arrange corrupt deals that also benefited the Confederates. Because military and guerrilla raids were continually burning cotton bales, many farmers chose to sell their cotton as fast as possible, but only at the lower price offered by the speculators.[101]

Ulysses S. Grant. *Library of Congress.*

The situation was so chaotic that a correspondent with the *Chicago Tribune* described, in his article on December 18, 1862, what it was like when General Grant was in Holly Springs, Mississippi: "If ever a community were insane, or afflicted with a disgusting moral malady, it is the crowds of speculators and vagrants which have congregated at Holly Springs to deal in cotton—they have 'cotton' on the brain—every one of them."[102]

General Grant was plagued with constant requests for permits and transportation requests from the speculators, and he believed that many of them were carrying vital military intelligence and trading with gold to the Confederates when they were traveling back and forth from the enemy lines. Grant felt that guarding the shipments also demoralized his troops because of the many unscrupulous dealings that were occurring everywhere, including with his soldiers.[103]

General William Tecumseh Sherman believed that the speculators were hurting the war effort, and he often referred to them as the "Jews and speculators" in his letters. In one of them, on July 31, 1862, he stated, "They were nearly out of bacon and salt meat, but the desire of our people to trade has soon supplied this. Cincinnati has sent enough salt to supply all their army for six months. In like manner the Jews and speculators have sent in enough gold to get all the cartridges necessary, so the two wants of the army are supplied, a whole year lost to the war, and some Jews and speculators have made ten per cent profit. Of course our lives are nothing in the scales of profit with our commercial people. The buying of cotton by the people of the South was one act of folly, but our buying the refuse of them for gold and especially shipping salt, which from scarcity has risen to $100 a barrel, is a greater act of folly."[104]

Adding to General Grant's problems, many soldiers saw the opportunity of making good money too good to pass up, entering into illicit dealings

Honorable Edwin Stanton. *Library of Congress.*

with speculators. In one account, an agent of the War Department and the future assistant secretary of war, Charles A. Dana, wrote a letter on January 21, 1863, in Memphis to Edwin M. Stanton, the secretary of war, regarding the problem: "Every colonel, captain, or quartermaster is in secret partnership with some operator in cotton; every soldier dreams of adding a bale of cotton to his monthly pay. I had no conception of the extent of this evil until I came and saw for myself. Besides, the resources of the rebels are inordinately increased from this source. Plenty of cotton is brought in from beyond our lines, especially by the agency of Jewish traders, who pay for it ostensibly in Treasury notes, but really in gold."[105]

General Grant wrote to Christopher P. Wolcott, the assistant secretary of war in Washington, D.C., on December 17, telling him how he had been expelling some of the Jewish speculators from his department, but they kept coming, with their "carpet-sacks," no matter what he did to try to stop the constant traffic. He said that the "Jews seem to be a privileged class that can travel everywhere. They will land at any wood-yard on the river and make their way through the country. If not permitted to buy cotton themselves they will act as agents for some one else, who will be at a military post with a Treasury permit to receive cotton and pay for it in Treasury notes which the Jew will buy up at an agreed rate, paying gold."[106]

General Grant told Wolcott that he believed the answer was for the government to buy up all the cotton at a fixed rate and then send it to Cairo, St. Louis or anywhere else away from him, so that "all traders (they are a curse to the army) might be expelled."[107]

The resentment the Union army had to the cotton trade speculators continued to grow after continually dealing with unscrupulous traders, and many officers' bigotry began to show toward the Jews in general by stereotyping all of them into this persona they were so used to seeing around the headquarters of their camps. General Grant was one of them, and even though not all of the speculators were Jewish, this did not deter their animosity against the Jewish traders.[108]

While preparing to move out in his first campaign to take Vicksburg, Mississippi, General Grant sent a telegraph from Lagrange, Tennessee, on November 9, 1862, to Major General Steven A. Hurlbut ordering him to "[r] efuse all permits to come south of Jackson for the present...The Isrealites [*sic*] especially should be kept out."[109]

In mid-December, General Grant's father, Jesse Grant, visited his son's headquarters in Mississippi, and traveling with him were the Mack brothers—Harman, Henry and Simon—who were influential Jewish clothing manufacturers from Cincinnati, Ohio. Grant's father was in a secret partnership with them to gain a permit to purchase cotton, along with a means to transport the cotton to New York, and the agreement was that he would travel with them to his son's headquarters to act as their agent for a fourth of the cut. But they were completely unaware of all of the problems that cotton had been for the younger Grant. He exploded in anger at his father and the Mack brothers when he first learned of the plan, and according to a witness present when this occurred, journalist Sylvanus Cadwallader from the *Chicago Times*, Grant erupted at his father's attempt to profit from his position in the army, while also raging at the brothers for trying to involve his father in their nefarious and unworthy plan. He immediately sent the brothers home on the first train north, and it was shortly after this event that General Orders No. 11 was issued, on December 17, 1862.[110]

General Grant's chief of staff, Lieutenant Colonel John A. Rawlins, objected to the order as it was being prepared and told the general that it could be seen as discriminatory toward the Jews, but this did not deter Grant, who told him, "Well, they can countermand this from Washington if they like, but we will issue it anyhow."[111]

When the order was first issued, four military officers sent messages to General Grant's headquarters in an attempt to determine if the order included the Jewish sutlers who were following the military camps. Because the sutlers, merchants and peddlers who followed the camps and sold non-military day-to-day goods such as food, tobacco, liquor and clothing offered a service that was good for their soldiers' morale, the officers questioned the need to expel the Jewish traders and held off following the order until they received an answer to their queries.[112]

Left: General John A. Rawlins. *Library of Congress.*

Right: Mr. Jesse Grant. *Library of Congress.*

In the *Israelite* newspaper from Cincinnati, Ohio, on January 23, 1863, it was reported that General Jeremiah Sullivan, at Jackson, Tennessee, refused to enforce the unjust order when he first read it, and he was said to have stated that he "thought he was an officer of the army and not of the church."[113]

Three days later, as General Grant was south preparing for a possible attack on Vicksburg from northern Mississippi, Confederate major general Earl Van Dorn attacked Grant's supply lines at Holly Springs, Mississippi, capturing two thousand soldiers, burning a large amount of Union rations and causing fifty miles of damage to the rail and telegraph. Because of this raid, Grant's communications were knocked down and unreliable for weeks, contributing to the slow reactions to implementing the order.[114]

At the same time, General Nathan Bedford Forrest, commanding his force of cavalry in the district around Memphis, attacked posts and the railroad lines between Jackson, Tennessee, and Columbus, Kentucky. These two raids caused General Grant to determine that attacking Vicksburg from northern Mississippi was not possible because of the inability to protect the long supply lines to the front.[115]

Another issue that may have caused confusion was that of the Jewish soldiers and officers in the Union army, especially those under the command of General Grant. Were they to be banned as well from Grant's theater of operations? Captain Philip Trounstine of the Fifth Ohio Cavalry was so incensed at the order that he resigned his commission, saying that he could not "help feeling, that as I owe filial affection to my parents, Devotion to my Religion, and a deep regard for the opinion of my friends and feeling that I can no longer, bear the Taunts and malice, of those to whom my religious opinions are known, brought on by the effect that, that order has instilled into their minds. I herewith respectfully tender you my immediate and unconditional resignation."[116]

General Nathan B. Forrest. *Library of Congress.*

ENFORCING THE ORDER

Even though the order was slow getting out, there were a few cases where Jews were mistreated within the Holly Springs Headquarters region; where one group was refused rail transportation to Memphis, forcing them to trek on foot forty miles to the city; and where another group was imprisoned, fined and sent on a military train to Jackson, Tennessee, where they received orders to promptly leave the military district.[117]

Outside General Grant's immediate headquarters region, there were no reported occurrences of the order, except in Paducah, Kentucky, when it was finally received to the desk of Captain L.J. Waddell, Paducah's provost marshal, and when he read the order, he implemented it to the fullest extent by preparing orders for the removal of thirty Jewish men and their families in the city. As provost marshal, Waddell's role was to police the city of Paducah for the Union army under the orders of Grant, and he followed the order to the letter, whereas other officers in other areas disregarded the command to expel the Jews.[118]

Kaskel was summoned to the office of Captain Waddell on Sunday, December 28, 1862, and handed an order to leave the city:

OFFICE OF PROVOST MARSHAL
Paducah, Ky., December 28, 1862

C.J. Kaskel—Sir: In pursuance of General Order No 11, issued from General Grant's headquarters, you are hereby ordered to leave the city of Paducah, Kentucky, within twenty-four hours after receiving this order.

By order,
L.J. WADDELL,
Captain and Provost Marshal[119]

The other Jewish men of Paducah were also given orders to leave the military district within twenty-four hours, even though two of the men were formerly Union soldiers, so they all began hurried preparations for leaving the city. But Kaskel was outraged with the order and was not going to let this injustice go without a fight.[120] Kaskel and several other families decided that the best way to fight the order was to go to the top, and they hurriedly sent a telegram to President Abraham Lincoln describing what happened:[121]

PADUCAH, KY., December 29, 1862.
Hon. ABRAHAM LINCOLN,
President of the United States:

General Orders, No. 11, issued by General Grant at Oxford, Miss., December the 17th, commands all post commanders to expel all Jews, without distinction, within twenty-four hours, from his entire department. The undersigned, good and loyal citizens of the United States and residents of this town for many years, engaged in legitimate business as merchants, feel greatly insulted and outraged by this inhuman order, the carrying out of which would be the grossest violation of the Constitution and our rights as good citizens under it, and would place us, besides a large number of other Jewish families of this town, as outlaws before the whole world. We respectfully ask your immediate attention to this enormous outrage on all law and humanity, and pray for your effectual and immediate interposition. We would respectfully refer you to the post commander and post adjutant as to our loyalty, and to all respectable citizens of this community as to our standing citizens and merchants. We respectfully ask for immediate instructions to be sent to the commander of this post.

D. WOLFF & BROS.
C.F. KASKELL [C.J. KASKEL].
J.W. KASWELL [KASKEL].

Their telegram was received in Washington, and General Halleck, who was now the general-in-chief of all the Union armies, endorsed it on December 31. But it was either ignored or lost before it could reach President Lincoln. It could have been overlooked because Lincoln and his staff were busy preparing the Emancipation Proclamation, which was issued on January 1, 1863.[122]

In their rush to leave the city, there were stories of how one baby was nearly left behind and how two elderly sick women were allowed to stay with neighbors to care for them. Also, there is folklore in Paducah that tells the story of a Union soldier knocking on the door of a Jewish resident. When he asked them who they were, the resident replied, "tailor," in a heavy German accent; the soldier replied, "Sorry to bother you, Mr. Taylor, but I'm looking for Jews."[123]

After leaving Paducah on the steamship *Charley Bowen* on the Ohio River, first to Cairo, Illinois, and then up to Cincinnati, Ohio, Kaskel quickly wrote out his account and sent telegrams to many leading members of the American Jewish community and to the press. It was picked up by the Associated Press and printed on December 30, 1862. He described his situation of being expelled from his home and community, stating that he was a "peaceable, law abiding citizen, pursuing my legitimate business at Paducah, Kentucky, where I have been a resident for nearly four years, have been driven from my home, my business, and all that is dear to me, at the short notice of twenty-four hours; not for any crime committed, but simply because I was born of Jewish parents."[124]

Kaskel pleaded with the press to help spread the news of the order by saying, "On my way to Washington, in order to get this most outrageous and inhuman order of Major General Grant countermanded, I ask you, gentleman, to lend the powerful aid of the press to the suffering cause of outraged humanity; to blot out as quick as possible this stain on our national honor, and to show the world that the American people, as a nation, brand the author of that infamous order as unworthy of their respect and confidence."[125]

Kaskel arrived in Cincinnati, Ohio, and only stayed for a short time, long enough to talk to the leaders of the Jewish community in the city to collect letters of recommendation, before heading out to Washington, D.C., to speak to Lincoln personally, as well as with one of the Wolff brothers who was expelled from Paducah.[126]

Arriving in Washington on January 3, 1863, with letters of recommendation from Max Lilienthal, a rabbi and educator in Cincinnati,

Honorable John A. Gurley, Ohio. NARA—528705. *Wikimedia Commons.*

and Daniel Wolf, a respected merchant from the same city, Kaskel went to speak to Congressman John A. Gurley of Cincinnati, Ohio, a Republican who had recently lost his reelection campaign but was friends with the Jewish leaders in Cincinnati and had access to the president.[127]

Kaskel explained what had happened, and Gurley took him to go see President Lincoln, arriving at dusk. There is one account of the meeting between the two, though without authenticity to the story, that when the president greeted them and learned what happened, he remarked, "And so, the children of Israel were driven from the happy land of Canaan?" "Yes," Kaskel responded, "and that is why we have come unto Father Abraham's bosom, asking protection." "And this protection," Lincoln declared, "they shall have at once."[128]

After explaining the full situation to the president, Lincoln told him that he had not been told about the order removing the Jews from the district, and he immediately penned an order revoking General Orders No. 11 and sent a message to General Halleck to rescind the order, telling Kaskel that he could go home—by the time he reached Paducah, the order would be rescinded.[129]

General Halleck sent Lincoln's directive to Grant the next day:[130]

> *WAR DEPARTMENT,*
> *Washington, January 4, 1863.*
> *Major-General GRANT,*
> *Holly Springs, Miss.:*
>
> *A paper purporting to be General Orders, No. 11, issued by you December 17, has been presented here. By its terms it expels all Jews from your department. If such an order has been issued, it will be immediately revoked.*
>
> *H.W. HALLECK*
> *General-In-Chief.*

Kaskel immediately headed back to Paducah that evening, and he arrived back in the city before Lincoln's revoking of General Orders No. 11 became known to the officers, most likely due to the communications problems that General Grant was still experiencing. When his presence in the city was discovered by the post commander, he was asked whose orders allowed him to return, and the emphatic response from Kaskel was, "By order of the President of the United States."[131]

Because the order was not immediately revoked in General Grant's reports, Lincoln felt that he was due an explanation, to maintain a good relationship with Grant, so General Halleck had Colonel John C. Kelton write an unofficial message to Grant on January 5 explaining that the wording of his order excluded a whole class of people instead "of certain obnoxious individuals." The message added, "Had the word 'pedler' been inserted after Jew I do not suppose any exception would have been taken to the order. Several officers and a number of enlisted men in your Dept are Jews. A Govr of one of the Western states is a Jew."[132]

General Henry W. Halleck. *Library of Congress.*

It was two days later, after General Halleck's message to revoke the order, when Grant's office transmitted the order of recall, on January 6, nearly three weeks after it was first issued. General Grant's new order was short and to the point, stating, "By direction of General-in-Chief of the Army, at Washington, the general order from these headquarters expelling Jews from the department is hereby revoked." Later, on January 21, Halleck sent another message to Grant officially to clarify the thoughts of President Lincoln, saying that he had no objection to his order expelling traders and Jewish peddlers and that he thought that was the true reason for the order, but because it expelled an entire religious class, including soldiers in the ranks, the president "deemed it necessary to revoke it."[133]

After the high numbers of casualties inflicted on the Union soldiers at the Battle of Shiloh on April 6 and 7, 1862, Lincoln had many requests to remove General Grant from command, claiming that he was incompetent as a commander, with accusations of heavy drinking, and that it was only the last-minute arrival of General Don Carlos Buell that saved him from a complete military disaster. The president told them that he could not spare the general because "he fights," and the same could be true regarding General Orders No. 11, where Lincoln may have believed that he needed to keep an eye on Grant. But he wanted no distractions to interfere with the military campaigns against the Confederate stronghold on the Mississippi River at Vicksburg, Mississippi.[134]

While Kaskel was making his way to talk to the president in Washington, delegations of Jewish leaders from Cincinnati, Ohio, and Louisville, Kentucky, were preparing to travel to Washington to talk with the president concerning General Orders No. 11. The Cincinnati group included Rabbis Max Lilienthal and Isaac Mayer Wise, the editor of the *Israelite* newspaper, along with lawyer Edgar M. Johnson, and the Louisville group included lawyer Martin Bijur and Abraham Goldsmith, a merchant from Paducah. While en route to the Capitol, they learned that Kaskel was successful in getting the order revoked, but they continued on regardless, to thank the president in person for his decisive action on the matter.[135]

When they arrived in Washington, they met Congressman Gurley, as Kaskel had done, and received the same prompt invitation to go and speak to the president; in fact, they did not have time to even change out of their traveling clothes before heading out. Rabbi Isaac Wise wrote an account in the *Israelite* of the meeting with President Lincoln on January 16, 1863:[136]

> *Having expressed our thanks for the promptness and dispatch in revoking General Grant's order, the President gave utterance to his surprise that Grant should have issued so ridiculous an order, and added—"to condemn a class is, to say the least, to wrong the good with the bad. I do not like to hear a class or nationality condemned on account of a few sinners." The President, we must confess, fully illustrated to us and convinced us that he knows of no distinction between Jew and Gentile, that he feels no prejudice against any nationality, and that he by no means will allow that a citizen in any wise be wronged on account of his place of birth or religious confession.*

After the Order

On January 5, 1863, Democrat senator and former governor of Kentucky Lazarus Powell brought up a resolution in the Senate to condemn General Grant's order, and on January 9, he brought with him documents from residents of Paducah showing that they had been expelled from the city. Powell concluded that Grant "might just as well expel the Baptists, or the Methodists, or the Episcopalians, or the Catholics, as a class, as to expel the Jews. All are alike protected in the enjoyment of their religion by the Constitution of our country." Republican senators John Hale and Charles Sumner succeeded in getting the resolution tabled, which ended the discussion in the Senate; a resolution in the House of Representatives was also attempted, but it met the same lack of success as in the Senate.[137]

After General Grant's victory at the Battle of Vicksburg on July 4, 1863, the calls for his dismissal by President Lincoln quieted, and Grant was considered a hero thereafter for the Union cause. That is, until Grant decided to run for

Honorable Lazarus W. Powell. *Library of Congress.*

president of the United States in 1868. General Orders No. 11 became a campaign issue in the election, and throughout it all, he never said a word about the order. But he did have John Rawlins issue a statement regarding the order in the *New York Times* on June 22, 1868, that noted, "The idea that it was issued on account of the religion of the Jews cannot be seriously entertained by any one who knows the General's steadfast adherence to the principles of American liberty and religious toleration." Grant went on to win the presidency by more than 300,000 votes and more than enough electoral votes, but during the election, there were Jewish leaders who were both for and against the general.[138]

One of the most noticeable actions of President Grant during his presidency was that he appointed more Jews to public office than any president before him, and he gained many Jewish friends who were quick to speak out in favor of his presidency. It appears that he went out of way to wipe away the memory of General Orders No. 11—"that obnoxious order," as his wife, Julia Dent Grant, referred to it.[139]

Cesar Kaskel remained in Paducah for only a short time after the war, moving to New York City and opening a high-end clothing business afterward. Even though he did not become an outspoken Jewish leader like Isaac Wise or Simon Wolf, his swift action and audacity helped put an end to General Orders No. 11. One thing that is fairly certain is that he would have had a wonderful story to tell his customers.[140]

Chapter 5

The Battle of Paducah

An Attack May Be Coming: March 20–24, 1864

After the initial excitement of Confederate general Polk invading Kentucky to take Hickman and Columbus, General Grant's taking of Paducah and the Union successes in the Battles of Fort Henry and Fort Donelson, the region went through the adjustment of being occupied by the Union army. Because of this, many Confederate sympathizers conducted illegal trade with the Confederate army.

Both pro-Confederate and pro-Union groups formed bands of guerrilla fighters, also called "bushwhackers" over in Missouri, using guerrilla warfare tactics. These groups became prevalent in the area, causing much death and hardship. There were guerrillas who did not discriminate against Confederate sympathizer or unionist, using the war was a means for getting rich off stolen merchandise. They were all vicious in the way they attacked and robbed the citizens of the Jackson Purchase, and this was one of the direct causes for much of the animosity in the region, creating hatreds and a reason for revenge attacks as a way of life for many.

On July 31, 1863, General Ambrose Burnside declared martial law in Kentucky "for the purpose only of protecting the rights of loyal citizens and the freedom of election," so if anyone was considered disloyal to the Union, they could not vote and they needed the approval from the military to prove they were good Union citizens to do so. This offended many of the secessionists in the Jackson Purchase region because there were many

Confederate sympathizers. To add to their insult, Federal officials were given the power to control how much material anyone could have on hand at any given time if the area was deemed a target for raiders, and Federal treasury agents determined that no one could keep more than two months' supply of goods, which directly affected the profits from many of the wholesale merchants in the area.[141]

The importance of Paducah was its proximity to the confluence of the Tennessee and Ohio Rivers, where crucial supply lanes could be blocked and disrupting access to these would stop the military supplies being shipped on the rivers to the front, which could cause considerable damage to the Union war effort if they could not reach their destination. Alternate methods of transportation would have to be employed, and this could create life-threatening delays for the Union army.

In the week before the Battle of Paducah occurred, rumors were rampant about General Nathan Bedford Forrest bringing his large force of cavalry north to attack either Columbus or Paducah, but over the many months of continuous guerrilla activity in the region, the city had become accustomed to warnings of a possible attack, and many residents in the city did not believe that an attack would occur.[142]

General Forrest had good reason to head north into western Tennessee and Kentucky; the main objective was to try to slow down the soldiers in General Sherman's planned attack of Atlanta by disrupting the supply lines from the rivers and railroad in Paducah, but another reason was to obtain needed supplies and new recruits for his regiments because there were many sympathizers in the area to help his army.[143]

It was a time of much tribulation in the area, with the disruption of trade that was hurting the residents economically, whether they were secessionist or unionist alike; Confederate guerrillas were also a big concern to the Union commanders in the area for many months before the Battle of Paducah occurred. Colonel Stephen G. Hicks communicated to command on March 23, 1864, that "[t]hirty-five guerrillas met railroad train at Mayfield yesterday; killed one negro man and shot several times at a Union man, who escaped. No Union man can go out of this place with safety in that direction. The interior is full of guerrillas."[144]

In another report, wired on March 22, 1864, Colonel William H. Lawrence, of the Thirty-fourth New Jersey Infantry and posted in Columbus, Kentucky, described the attacks, vandalism and theft that occurred in Fancy Farm, Kentucky: "Julian Sanderson, mail carrier between Columbus and Mayfield, reports that the postmaster at Fancy

Farms, 10 miles south of Mayfield, was shot this morning; also the Catholic chapel at that place destroyed; that Willet & Boswell's store was entered, taking all their goods. They number about 50 men, and have taken off some 4 or 5 citizens as prisoners."[145]

The feeling was mutual from the Confederate soldiers and sympathizers concerning the "Home-Guard" guerrilla activity that was used by the Union army for information. Henry George, a Confederate soldier in the Seventh Kentucky Mounted Infantry, had this to say about the pro-Union guerrilla group: "From the middle to the close of the war portions of Kentucky and Tennessee were infested with gangs of robbers and murderers calling themselves 'Home Guards,' most of whom had some sort of affiliation with the Federal armies, and if they did not act under orders from the Federal commanders they certainly made no effort to restrain them."[146]

General Forrest may also have wanted to attack the Union forts because former slaves were being recruited in Paducah to be soldiers, and he believed they should always be considered as property; if any African American soldiers were captured, they would have been brought back to their owners or sold in the slave market, but the newly recruited soldiers knew that they would probably suffer torture and death if they were captured.[147]

A message was received in Paducah from Colonel Hicks's superior, General Mason Brayman, at Columbus, telling him that Union City fell at 11:00 a.m. on March 24, 1864, and that it was a possibility that Paducah would be attacked. Colonel Hicks had no way of knowing exactly what General Forrest's plan was, but he made his plans and instructed his officers to be ready for any eventuality.[148]

HOSPITAL NO. 2: MARCH 20–24, 1864

After the Battle of Shiloh on April 6, 1862, Paducah became an important area for the creation of many hospitals to help the vast numbers of sick and wounded being shipped down the Tennessee River, away from the front lines in the south. Many places in Paducah were used as makeshift hospitals, including the Baptist, Christian, Episcopal, Methodist and Presbyterian churches, along with the Female Seminary, the courthouse and other public and private buildings.[149]

Nurse Jennie Fyfe, from Lansing, Michigan, arrived in the city on the evening of March 19, 1864, to work at Paducah Hospital No. 2 by helping the injured in the war, and it is to our good fortune that she wrote letters to her sister, Nell Fyfe, that have been preserved, detailing the life and conditions of the area during this time of the Civil War. On the morning of March 20, she noted that Paducah was "a larger place than I had supposed. About ten thousand inhabitants they tell me. Lighted with gas &c, &c. But it is chill here now, very chill. Few ladies are seen upon the streets, but a great many soldiers. The place is protected by gunboats & a fort."[150]

When she arrived to the hospital, she was told by the nurses that they had a scare the night before about fears that Paducah was going to be attacked from guerrillas, which were said to be in large numbers down in Mayfield, a town to the south that is connected by the railroad in the city. She was told in case the town was attacked to be prepared because the Union troops had standing orders to fire upon the city to prevent the commissary stores from falling into the hands of the enemy. But she was also told that since there were so many secessionists in the city, they would use their influence against an assault on the city because they would lose their property as well, just as those who favored the Union cause would if an attack were to take place.[151]

On Thursday, March 24, a day before the battle, Fyfe saw how rumor of an attack was growing in the city, but little was heeded to prepare for its eventuality; she wrote to her sister explaining how the day occurred:

> *Thursday, March 24th we were surprised by the ringing of the alarm bell, calling the Union League together. The Enemy were said to be coming upon us yet no one seemed alarmed. & things moved on quietly as usual. Soon after dinner it again sounded & all went immediately to the Hall. A little excitement prevailed for awhile but died away as evening approached. We ladies walked out to the Fort to see something of the stir. The guns were all mounted there, & the gun Boats in readiness for an attack but after all, none among us seemed to think but we were all safe. I could not sleep that night, though I kept very quiet about, the rest seemed so fearless & free from alarm.*[152]

Fort Anderson: Early Morning

The fort was full of activity early in the morning, sending out scouts to watch for General Forrest's army and gathering everything essential from the posts in the city to bring inside the fort. Major James Chapman received orders to maintain his command in readiness at his post inside the city, and if he were to encounter any trouble, he was to move all of his men immediately to the fort.[153]

The fort was located across from Hospital Street, today's Martin Luther King Jr. Drive, around Fourth Street, and Trimble Street, today's Park Avenue, ended at the west wall of the fort. It was approximately four hundred feet long and four hundred feet wide, surrounded by a deep ditch filled with water, creating a moat. Colonel Hicks had a total of 665 men in his command at the fort: 274 men from the 1st Kentucky Heavy Artillery, commanded by Lieutenant R.D. Cunningham; 271 from the 16th Kentucky Cavalry, commanded by Major Barnes; and 120 from the 122nd Illinois Infantry, commanded by Major J.F. Chapman.[154]

The 122nd Illinois Infantry was the only regiment in the fort that had actual combat experience. The 16th Kentucky Cavalry was created on February 15, 1864, with Paducah being the recruitment center for the regiment, and the 1st Kentucky Heavy Artillery was composed of the newly recruited African American soldiers, beginning on February 27, 1864—some being former

A model of Fort Anderson at the Lloyd Tilghman House and Civil War Museum. *Photo by author.*

slaves of Paducah residents who were not too happy with the loss. When a slave enlisted, they were free, along with their families, but this also caused a large amount of resentment from the former slave owners, making them targets for Confederate soldiers, and if they were captured, they could expect death or a return to slavery.[155]

Because the fort was built so close to the properties on the north side of the city, Fort Anderson was ringed closely by many houses on the streets, and this was noticed early in the occupation of Paducah, when the fort was being built. While many homes and buildings near the fort were labeled early on as being hazardous to the soldiers in the fort if occupied by the enemy, nothing was done to eliminate the threat to the fort.[156]

HOSPITAL NO. 2: 2:00 P.M.–6:00 P.M.

At about 2:00 p.m., word reached Hospital No. 2 that a courier was sent to Colonel Hicks telling him that the Confederate army was, in fact, approaching Paducah, and when Fyfe went to look out of the upstairs window, she saw the horde coming in from the outskirts of town. She and the other nurses dressed themselves for an emergency and then went to their wards. "Our able bodied men save the Steward, druggist & two nurses," Fyfe wrote later, "had gone to the fort immediately on the receipt of the news of the enemy's coming." Fyfe was one of the two nurses who stayed to take care of the wounded soldiers who could not make it to the fort.[157]

An hour later, Fyfe was talking with one of the men left in her ward when she first saw the Confederate soldiers surrounding the hospital, and as she went to look out of the window, one soldier had his pistol drawn ready to fire. She hurried away from the window, and the nurses were ordered to go below into the cellar. While she was heading downstairs, she heard the boom of the cannons from the fort and the gunboats firing. Immediately after hearing this, the doors were kicked open, and Confederate soldiers and officers began entering the hospital and demanding surrender.[158]

She and the others surrendered—their group consisted of herself, the steward, the druggist, one lame nurse using crutches and the patients who could not make it to the fort. The Confederates immediately began plundering everything useful, beginning by first entering the office and then taking all of the medicines. They began ordering the Union soldiers who could walk to help move the boxes of looted supplies out to the carts, and

Fyfe noted later that "it made our blood boil a little to see them perform & hear them command our men—They were exceedingly polite to us ladies, during all of their stay here, but became rough & profane, to the men generally. After they had taken the medicines they proceeded to the closets where the soldiers knapsacks & clothing were, Dressed themselves in our mens clothes, took what knapsacks they could carry & whatever else they had time & place for."[159]

Fyfe recounted an incident in one of her letters to her sister about how a Confederate officer commanded the steward to harness the horses and then put them before the ambulance, but the steward told the officer that he would not do it. The officer then turned his attention to one of his men and ordered him to harness the horses and drive them away.[160]

Fyfe noted that at least fifty Confederates were in the ward and house pillaging, and she observed that they "presented a ludicrous appearance dressed in all sorts of colored clothing, their horses laden with cloths of all kind, shawls, silks, &c. &c."[161]

In one anecdote that Fyfe described later, the steward and the druggist disappeared while the Confederates were still plundering the hospital, but she and the other nurse knew where they were hiding (up in the cupola of the hospital). She said that she had some sport in sending up to them food, candles, matches and cigars wrapped in a sheet.[162]

During the hospital's occupation by the Confederates, Fyfe noted that she saw General Forrest standing in the backyard, close to the house, and she described him as being a "fine looking man, but how deceiving his looks." He then gave orders to take all the prisoners who could walk and move them to an officer to be questioned. It was around 6:00 p.m. when the Confederates left the hospital, and Jennie Fyfe was not sure if they would return or not.[163]

THE BATTLE

On Friday morning, Major James Chapman, with members of his 122nd Illinois Infantry, sent some of his scouts to watch the approaches from Mayfield Road, outside the city, to check for any advances from General Forrest's army. At 2:00 p.m., he got a report saying that the Confederate army was three miles from the city, at which point he immediately formed his men and marched them back double-time to the fort, as were his orders. Once back into the fort, Chapman had his men take their assigned positions manning the wall. He stated later in his official report that he "formed my command on the west side of the front, with my right and left respectively resting near two 24-pounder siege guns, while in my center was a 24-pounder howitzer. In this position I awaited the approach of the enemy."[164]

Colonel Stephen G. Hicks had one group of scouts come back to the fort at noon saying that the enemy was not seen, but he sent them out again. Three miles from town, they encountered the advance guard for Forrest's army, which fired upon them. They immediately fell back to town, raising the alarms, and within minutes, the Confederates were driving in the Federal pickets and skirmishing fire was being reported, with the Confederates firing into the backs of his retreating men. Hicks immediately ordered everyone back to the fort for the protection of its walls. Earlier, the fort received further protection when the USS *Peosta*, a tin-clad gunboat, arrived at 12:00 p.m., joining the USS *Paw Paw*, which was already stationed at Paducah.[165]

When the Confederates entered the city, Private J.V. Grief, Paducah resident and a soldier in the Third Kentucky Mounted Infantry, Company D, stated that the regiment reached the Federal picket line at Eden's Hill at 2:10 p.m. and that it entered the city on Mayfield Road, where Guthrie and Seventeenth Street meet today, under the command of Lieutenant Jarrett and Colonel Albert P. Thompson. Before the war began, Thompson was a prominent lawyer in Paducah and served as McCracken County's commonwealth's attorney. It was decided earlier in the morning from Mayfield that Company D, of the Third Kentucky, would be allowed to join in the vanguard of the army since it knew the land and the people, as this company consisted mostly of Paducah men who went off to serve as soldiers for the Confederate cause. They were originally the Third Kentucky Infantry, but after the Battle of Vicksburg, they were reassigned to General Forrest's cavalry as a mounted infantry regiment.[166]

When the Confederates reached the range of the cannons from the fort and the gunboats on the Ohio River, the Federal soldiers began firing all of their artillery at the approaching enemy. At 3:00 p.m., the Kentuckians were at what is today Fifteenth and Broadway, and Captain F.G. Terry, of the Confederate Eighth Kentucky Regiment, who was at this time serving as Colonel Thompson's ordnance officer, reported that Captain McGoodwin, the acting assistant adjutant general, was sent to General Abraham Buford to report the location of Colonel Thompson and ask for instructions. The order was returned telling them to "dismount your men and move against that fort, keeping your flanks well protected." Once they

"War Comes to Paducah"—section in the Lloyd Tilghman House and Civil War Museum. *Photo by author.*

were ready, they formed a line of battle and began marching immediately in the direction of the fort.[167]

Acting Volunteer Lieutenant Thomas Smith, who was commanding the USS *Peosta* in the absence of Lieutenant Commander James Shirk, who had just left on a ship to give a report at Cairo, Illinois, an hour earlier, reported that when the Confederates entered into firing range, he "steamed to the upper end of the city and opened on them with our starboard bow guns, the U.S.S. Paw Paw also opening at the same time. We then dropped down to the foot of Broadway and fired up the street."[168]

At this time, Union major Chapman saw that the Confederate infantry were "forming in my front at a distance of 1,000 yards. They very soon moved forward in three lines, with skirmishers in front. The latter took possession of some dwellings and the general hospital Numbers 1, and commenced firing at us through the windows and around the corners of the houses. From this position they were soon dislodged." Both the *Peosta* and the *Paw Paw* gunboats steamed next to the fort and provided aid in firing to help dislodge the Confederates from the buildings.[169]

At what became General Forrest's headquarters at Fifteenth and Broadway, six men from Company D were sent with a flag of truce to carry a message from Forrest to Colonel Hicks at the fort at about 4:00 p.m. In the book *Paducahans in History* by Fred G. Neuman, four names were recorded as the flag bearers: Charles Reed, John Brooks, Rufe Stevens and John Garrett. While the flag of truce was going up Broadway, the Third and Seventh Kentucky Regiments were advancing closer and began taking up positions to attack the fort, and the Eighth Kentucky Regiment was in the center of town, looting the commissary stores and searching for every horse, mule and wagon while also burning the quartermaster's supply depot building and the railroad depot, along with other important federal locations.[170]

When Colonel Hicks heard that a flag of truce was approaching, he immediately ordered the men in the fort and signaled the gunboats to cease firing; then he sent men out to meet the bearers with the flag to receive the message. The message read:

> *HEADQUARTERS FORREST'S CAVALRY CORPS,*
> *Paducah, Ky., March 25, 1864.*
>
> *Colonel HICKS,*
> *Commanding Federal Forces at Paducah:*
>
> *COLONEL: Having a force amply sufficient to carry your works and reduce the place, and in order to avoid the surrender of the fort and troops, with all public property. If you surrender, you shall be treated as prisoners of war; but if I have to storm your works, you may expect no quarter.*
>
> *N.B. FORREST,*
> *Major-General, Commanding Confederate Troops.*

In response, Colonel Hicks sent this reply to be delivered to the Confederate flag bearers:

> *HEADQUARTERS POST OF PADUCAH,*
> *Paducah, Ky., March 25, 1864.*
>
> *Major General N.B. FORREST,*
> *Commanding Confederate Forces:*

SIR: I have this moment received yours of this instant, in which you demand the unconditional surrender of the forces under my command. I can answer that I have been placed here by my Government to defend this post, and in this as well as all other orders from my superiors, I feel it to be my duty as an honorable office to obey. I must, therefore, respectfully decline surrendering as you may require.

S.G. HICKS
Colonel, Commanding Post.

Colonel Hicks noticed that while the flag of truce was near the fort, the Confederates were moving in and taking positions to attack the fort and gunboats while also trying to set up a small artillery battery. Once the reply message was returned at 4:30 p.m., the Confederates advanced, causing the fort and gunboats to open up fire on them; the engagement began in earnest. Union major Chapman saw that once the flag of truce returned, the Confederates advanced with a heavy force led by Colonel Thompson, and they "filled all the houses in reach of the fort, and opened a heavy fire from behind every obstacle that would afford them protection."[171]

As soon as the fort and the USS *Peosta* and USS *Paw Paw* gunboats began firing, Confederate general Buford, who was on the right flank in the east and south side of the city, re-formed the line so that the right was on Broadway, which he was commanding, and the left was on Cairo Road, commanded by Colonel Thompson. Buford left sharpshooters in the buildings next to the river on Front Street to fire on the gunboats in the river in an attempt to draw their fire away from the fort. The line continued to advance to be able to surround the fort, and it was maintained until they came to the more densely built part of the city, where the line was unable to be held, forcing the Confederates to form columns by regiments or companies to continue advancing on the fort down the streets. When they were within rifle range of the enemy, they were halted for a short time, about three hundred feet from the fort, making sure to protect themselves by getting behind houses and hiding in the alleys.[172]

Henry George, a Confederate soldier in the Seventh Kentucky Mounted Infantry and a soldier in the battle, stated that "they were moved forward again in the streets, the buildings on either side still preventing an advance in any sort of line until an open space was reached near the fort. While marching through the streets the command was under a constant and withering fire from the fort by both small arms and artillery. When out in open space, the lines were somewhat adjusted before the final charge was made. When within a short distance of the fort it was discovered that it was surrounded by a deep ditch with such perpendicular banks as to render crossing impossible."[173]

During one of the assaults on the fort, Ewell Hord, a young Confederate in Company D who was in the line next to and on the left of Paducahian J.V. Grief, asked if he could have help with loading his gun. Grief told him to load it himself, and the boy told him that he could not because he was wounded in the arm and not able to draw his rammer. Grief exclaimed to Hord, "Go to the rear, you fool! What better luck do you want? It gets you out of this!" With this, Hord went to the rear crying that no one would help him continue to fight.[174]

First Sergeant Thomas B. Fauntleroy, also in Confederate Company D of the Third and from Kevil, Kentucky, was with General Buford when the general rush occurred during the battle for the fort and was within forty yards of the parapet after the third attempted assault against the fort's walls when the attack was halted around 5:00 p.m. The gunboats were effectively firing their cannons directly up the streets to help clear them of the attacking soldiers, and the firing was intense up Trimble Street, where Colonel Thompson was in command. Union colonel Hicks stated that at this time, "They rallied and tried it again, and met the same fate. They made a third effort, but were forced to abandon their design."[175]

In a letter that he wrote home after the battle to his mother, Carpenter Mate Herbert Saunders noted that he was on the USS *Peosta* on the day of the battle; he stated that the ship kept "putting the shell and grape into them from all the guns that we could get to bear on them." Two hours into the battle, Saunders described how their "rifle men and some of the people of the town got into the buildings down by the river and pelled us with musket ball but we soon gave enough of that for we directed our whole fire on them at short range with shell grape and canister and soon fetched the bricks around their eyes."[176]

In another account that was in the *Indianapolis Journal*, George Vance, from Indianapolis, related his experiences in a letter home of the battle while serving on the USS *Peosta*. He recalled that the "first time the rebs charged up to the very ditch but fell back, having suffered severely. Our boat lay off abreast of the Fort, and we poured in a steady stream of shells. We worked seven guns, and I tell you we worked with a will. While the fighting was going on the women and children were being ferried across the river. I was really sorry to see the women driven around like so many sheep, but we could not stop to help them any."[177]

Vance stated that after driving the Confederates back from the fort, they began shelling the town because they were being shot at from "every window, hole, and corner on the levee, and it was just like a hail-storm for about half an hour. We of course could not work the guns on our upper deck, and it was dangerous loading even the guns behind the casemates, as we were so close to the buildings that the sharp-shooters could hit a port almost every time. We directed our shots at the buildings to drive them out; but actually the buildings would have to begin to crumble and fall before they would slacken their fire. Their fire was so accurate that I am minus a new pair of boots by it, and came near being minus a leg."[178]

Lieutenant Smith, in command of the USS *Peosta*, reported later how the musket fire coming from the buildings on Front Street became such a danger to his gunboat, saying, "In consequence of a heavy fire of musketry being directed upon us by sharpshooters in the buildings on Front Street, I reluctantly opened upon them, demolishing the City Hotel and brewery and setting several other buildings on fire."[179]

U.S. gunboat *Peosta*, Mississippi River fleet. *Library of Congress*.

After the last assault on the fort failed, Colonel Thompson was killed. J.V. Grief related that "a column of the Third Kentucky was entering the alley back of the present Frank Kirchhoff, Sr., property at Fifth and Trimble streets, a two-story brick farm house then occupied by Robert Crow. Colonel Thompson had halted and his horse stood a few feet east of the alley entrance, the horse facing the south with the fore hoofs in the gutter. The colonel was conversing with several officers and had his cap in the right hand held overhead at arm's length, when the cannonball struck him and the animal. The horse ran half a block to Sixth street and fell, and was later buried on the spot where a marker in the sidewalk determines the place where its gallant rider lost his life in sight of his home." In the fort, Colonel Hicks and Major Chapman both reported seeing the colonel fall.[180]

A retreat was called for the Confederates to fall back to the buildings, and many of the soldiers continued firing at the fort from the upper floors of the buildings nearest to the fort, behind them and also in any of the hollows that allowed them cover to fire. Colonel Crossland of the Seventh Kentucky Mounted Infantry took over command of the regiment after Colonel Thompson was killed, and he ordered his men to fall back behind the A.R. Lang's tobacco stemmery; shortly after this order, he was shot in the thigh with a musket ball. He was then succeeded in command by Lieutenant Colonel Holt.[181]

With the fighting being so intense, Colonel Hicks began to worry about his ammunition supply in the fort and on the gunboats. Out of thirty thousand rounds, he had already expended twenty-seven, and he ordered, in this emergency, that the "remainder to be equally distributed; the men to fix their bayonets; to make good use of the ammunition they had, and, when that was exhausted, to receive the enemy on the point of the bayonet feeling fully determined never to surrender while I had a man alive." Writing in his report later, Colonel Hicks noted, "When this order was repeated by the officers to their respective commands, it was received with loud shouts and cheers," but he also stated in the same report that the Confederate sharpshooters, after gaining possession of the houses around the fort, had killed and injured some of his gunners, many of whom were killed by being shot in the head.[182]

Major Chapman was also having a lot of trouble with the continuous shots coming from the sharpshooters in the houses, and when the fire began to slow down, he told his men to not fire unless they could see the enemy because of his concern for conserving ammunition.[183]

Nine sharpshooters from Company D were able to travel down Walnut Street (Sixth Street today), maneuvering around to reach a brick cottage owned by Gus Slusmeyer and located at 515 North Fourth Street. They entered the house to be able to shoot at the fort from one hundred feet away. J.V. Grief said that a cannon ball from the fort went through the house and knocked him down. He stated later, "On the enemy declining to surrender, we were ordered to advance in squads as sharpshooters and silence the guns. Lieut. Jarrett, with nine men, took a position protected by a frame cottage and we held our corner down. Our gun was never loaded after we got in position until the enemy succeeded in bringing to bear on us a gun from some other part of the fort. The ball came through the house and I was knocked down. As I fell I heard Lieut. Jarrett order the squad to get out. I don't know how long I was down, but when I got up all were gone."[184]

At the fort, Major Chapman saw the Confederates act as if they were going to renew the assault, but instead they began falling back at about 6:00 p.m., and he reported later, "Thus, after near three hours of hard fighting, the enemy was completely repulsed, leaving on the field 2 of their best generals, 1 captain, and 1 lieutenant, all killed. As they moved all the wounded and most of the dead, it was impossible for me to ascertain what was their loss in my immediate front. As several wagons were employed for near half an hour removing them, I concluded their loss was very heavy. Fifteen dead bodies were left on the ground near the fort."[185]

When the Confederates began withdrawing, the soldiers from the fort and the gunboats raised their guns and began shelling the horses that were left at Fifteenth and Broadway. One of the shells exploded, and a piece of shrapnel struck a cavalryman who was holding some of the horses in the hip. J.V. Grief stated that another piece of shrapnel passed between him and his horse, and he said that it ended up "cutting off my stirrup leather and breaking the horse's leg between the hock and the stifle joint. I rode the wounded man's horse out."[186]

After the Confederates withdrew from the fort, the main force moved a short distance outside Paducah in what is now known as the Hendron area to prepare a camp for the night, leaving a covering force of sharpshooters in a few of the buildings to hold the Federal soldiers within the fort for the night.[187]

At 10:30 p.m., Lieutenant Smith received reports that the Confederates were still destroying property, so he moved the USS *Peosta* up to the edge of town and began firing at where he thought they were located. Colonel Hicks later reported, "Toward dark the enemy took shelter behind houses, in rooms, and hollows, and kept up a scattering fire until 11:30 o'clock, when it entirely ceased, and the rebel general withdrew his command out of the range of my guns and went into camp for the night."[188]

HOSPITAL NO. 2: 6:00 P.M.–MIDNIGHT

After the Confederates left after 6:00 p.m., nurse Jennie Fyfe recalled that they kept expecting a return of what she called the "Rebel Horde." While they waited, women and children came by asking for a safe place, but they were questioned whether they were loyal or not. Asking this question may seem like a harsh act, but considering that time in Paducah, when there were two distinct groups, unionist and Confederate sympathizer, asking those wishing entry if they were loyal or not may have seemed very important for the U.S. army hospital to ask. At this time, no one knew for sure who was going to win the battle.[189]

Two shots came through the windows during the evening, causing many of the alarmed patients to crouch in the corners and under their beds. Later in the evening, a Confederate soldier entered Fyfe's ward and demanded that everyone hand over their money, but before the battle, the nurses were given the money and watches of the patients and hid them.[190]

One of the nurses from Hospital No. 1—which had been taken over early in the battle by the Confederates, who used it to fire at the fort from its windows because of its proximity—made it to Hospital No. 2 in the evening; she told them that the nurses were taken prisoner but that they all escaped during the battle. Considering how the nurses were treated respectfully at her hospital, Fyfe was grateful that she did not receive the same "scandalous treatment of the ladies of No. 1."[191]

THE RESIDENTS OF PADUCAH: 2:00 P.M.–11:00 P.M.

When the Confederates began encountering the picket line at Paducah, many of the residents started hearing musket fire in the distance coming toward them, and those who did not believe that the city would be attacked saw their worst fears coming true. Some residents left what they were doing and ran home to gather their families to find shelter from the coming battle, while others hid in their cellars or found hiding places to wait out the attack.

On March 25, 1927, Louis Kolb Sr. recounted that day's events in 1864 to the *News-Democrat* newspaper by describing how the advance rebel vanguard arrived at Eden's Hill at 2:10 p.m. and how Forrest's main body of his cavalry reached the area of Fifteenth and Broadway, dismounting his troops at 3:00 p.m. Kolb detailed how he and his wife finally made it to the riverbank at 5:00 p.m., and after finding a small boat, he "clung fast to the bottom of the boat while the firing was going on, near a woman with a bad case of smallpox, having less fear of contracting the disease than the shots from in and around the fort." He was able to get across the river at Brookport, Illinois, staying there until Sunday.[192]

In a *Louisville Journal* account on March 29, 1864, a Paducah resident gave his account of the day of the battle. The witness said the rebels arrived at 2:00 p.m. in the suburbs, and he thought that they have would have some time to get to safety. Within thirty minutes, though, he heard the first musket fire while making his way to provide safety for his family. After making it to the river, Quartermaster Captain J.A. Finley, staying cool under fire, remained to help load the scared residents onto a large wharf-boat of J.H. Fowler & Company, with at least one thousand people loaded on board, and after the Owens' ferryboat, called the *Blue Bird*, came alongside the wharf-boat to fasten them together. A coal barge, loaded with more residents, was also fastened to the ferryboat, and the trio made its way to the opposite shore, while the USS *Peosta* was firing over and around the group, causing "an awful tremor to seize our vitals."[193]

SATURDAY, MARCH 26, 1864

Before 7:00 a.m. the next morning, General Forrest was preparing to leave the property of George Schmidt, in the Hendron area outside Paducah, for Mayfield when he sent out his second flag of truce back to Paducah proposing an exchange of soldiers.[194] The message read as follows:[195]

HEADQUARTERS FORREST'S CAVALRY CORPS,
Near Paducah, Ky., March 26, 1864

Col. S.G. HICKS,
Commanding Federal Forces at Paducah, Ky.:

SIR: I understand you hold in your possession in the guard-house at Paducah a number of Confederate soldiers as prisoners of war. I have in my possession about 35 or 40 Federal soldiers who were captured here yesterday, and about 500 who were captured at Union City. I propose to exchange man for man, according to rank, so far as you may hold Confederate soldiers.

Respectfully,
N.B. Forrest,
Major-General, Commanding Confederate Forces.

When the army arrived in Mayfield, the Kentucky regiments were granted a furlough for a few days to go spend time to see family and homes, considering that most of the soldiers had not seen them since they enlisted back in 1861. It was noted in several sources that all of the Kentuckians returned to their units at Trenton, Tennessee, where they were to rendezvous, and when they returned, they had good mounts and comfortable clothing, along with many new recruits to join the regiments.[196]

Early in the morning at Fort Anderson, Colonel Hicks still viewed the enemy two and a half miles from the city making a demonstration of a possible attack, so he ordered Major Barnes of the Sixteenth Kentucky Cavalry to send out some of his squads to burn all of the houses that surrounded the fort, as the day before, many of his deaths and casualties occurred when the Confederate sharpshooters were occupying the upper stories of those homes and buildings—Colonel Hicks was going to remove those hazards endangering his troops at all cost.[197]

While Major Barnes was carrying out his order to burn the homes, General Forrest's flag of truce arrived, and Colonel Hicks replied as follows:[198]

HEADQUARTERS POST OF PADUCAH,
Paducah, Ky., March 26, 1864

Maj. Gen. N.B. FORREST,
Commanding Confederate Forces:

SIR: I have no power to make the exchange. If I had I would most cheerfully do it.

Very respectfully,
S.G. HICKS,
Colonel Fortieth Illinois Infantry, Commanding Post.

Even though some residents did not return until Sunday, some began being ferried back across the river early in the morning at dawn, and those property owners who had homes near the fort discovered that they were burning or going to be burned without a chance to remove any of their valuables. When some of the residents who had already returned asked if they could retrieve some of the furnishings, they were told that the order stated the homes must be burned immediately.[199]

In an account recorded by Fred Neuman in his book *Paducahans in History*, he described the story of how Colonel Thompson's body was removed from Trimble Street at 9:00 a.m.:

> *Colonel Thompson's mutilated body lay on Trimble street where he fell until the morning after the Battle of Paducah, when shortly before 9 o'clock John McClung and former Mayor D.A. Yeiser went to the site and gathered the remains, engaging a drayman to convey the torn body to the one-story frame building which then stood where the Post office now is located. Mr. McClung was a clerk at L.S. Trimble & Company's wholesale grocery and*

Confederate officer's uniform at the Lloyd Tilghman Museum and Civil War Museum. *Photo by author.*

> *Mr. Yeiser was then with the old Cope & Neel drug store on the north side of lower Broadway. They visited the place where the Colonel's body lay as soon as they heard of its being left in the disorder which for a few minutes followed his fall.*[200]

When some of the residents returned the next day, they found that a third of the town was destroyed, and everywhere they looked, many buildings still standing were riddled with holes from the shells of the two gunboats. One resident said that many "business and dwelling-houses have suffered greatly from the shells of the gunboats, prominent among which are the Continental Hotel, City Hotel, and Branch Bank of Louisville. The latter is almost a mass of ruins, with its entire contents. Cashier S.B. Hughes and family resided in the building, but, fortunately, had escaped."[201]

Over in Hospital No. 2, nurse Fyfe wrote home later saying that she saw another one of the nurses who had escaped from Hospital No. 1, which was burned down because of Colonel Hicks's order, due to its proximity to the fort. The nurse explained that once the fighting started, she hid behind a stump during the fighting, and when the truce flag came down Broadway and the firing ceased, she made her escape to the river and crossed in a boat. Fyfe said that she went out later to view the destruction in town and saw the place where Colonel Thompson fell and also the ruins of Hospital No. 1—six skeletons were found inside. Of the damage to the city, she wrote, "Some of the buildings burned were very fine; beautiful yards about them & every thing betokening wealth."[202]

The Importance of Paducah

Even though General Forrest succeeded in raiding Paducah's supplies and horses, while destroying the buildings used by the Federal army, militarily, the assault on the fort was a setback. The Union lost 14 men, 46 men were wounded and 40 were captured, but the Confederate losses are harder to define because many of the dead were either buried or taken back with the wounded to Mayfield and buried. Colonel Hicks estimated that 300 were killed and 1,000 to 1,200 were wounded from Forrest's cavalry, but reports during the Civil War were often exaggerated, so the numbers are most likely much lower. Whatever the case, Forrest lost a lot of men for just a raid.[203]

Confederate soldier Henry George later wrote that General Forrest stated that he "drove the enemy to their gunboats and fort, and held the town for ten hours; captured many stores and horses; burned sixty bales of cotton, one steamer and a dry dock, bringing out fifty prisoners. My loss, as far as known, is twenty-five killed and wounded, among them Colonel Thompson."[204]

The damage to Paducah was considerable, caused by both the fort's and gunboats' cannons and by the Confederate forces. General Forrest's soldiers burned the Union headquarters, the quartermaster and commissary building with all of its supplies, the railroad depot and a steamboat that was on the ways, the *Dacotah*. The Union forces burned down all of the buildings and homes near the fort, and the artillery burned and damaged many more buildings around the city, especially on the waterfront.[205]

It seems that General Forrest made a serious error in strategy when he ordered the attack on the fort, as the ditch, water and the size of the walls should not have been a surprise, and if they had done a little reconnaissance on the fort and its defenses before entering the city, the outcome may have ended differently, instead of rushing at full speed to assault its walls.[206]

It could be that General Forrest knew strategically that he could not stay long before more gunboats and troops arrived to relieve the fort; this could explain why he decided to move his army back to Mayfield, but if he had continued the assault that morning, considering the fort's ammunition was desperately low, they could have possibly been able to overpower the Union soldiers when their ammunition ran out. However, because his force was a cavalry, Forrest probably knew that he did not have the necessary equipment and artillery to continue occupying Paducah, especially since he would not have the supply line needed to stay.

It was questioned later about who ordered the assault on the fort. General Forrest's biographers later pushed the narrative that Colonel Thompson assaulted the fort on his own initiative, saying that Forrest ordered him to just hold the enemy soldiers in the fort. But Forrest was the kind of general who demanded respect, so many believe that Thompson was indeed acting on orders to attack. It could be possible that Forrest allowed the assault to continue after the ditch and walls were seen for the first time, either because he thought that a lightning-strike attack could win the day or because he was affording the chance for Thompson to take his hometown for the South.[207]

Another reason why the assault on the fort was so intense could also be the fact that former African American slaves from Paducah were manning the walls of the fort, and General Forrest and his men wanted to send a message to all slaves who may have been thinking about abandoning their masters to join the Union army. Evidence to this fact can be shown by Forrest's attack on Fort Pillow in Tennessee on April 12, 1864, where nearly all of the African American soldiers manning the fort were tortured and killed following the surrender. If Fort Anderson had fallen to the Confederates, it is very possible that the African American soldiers would have had the same fate.[208]

If the fort was destroyed and the garrison killed or captured, this would have disrupted the supplies getting to Chattanooga from the Tennessee River to help the attack on Atlanta that was fought on July 22, 1864. If it was General Forrest's goal to slow down General Sherman's march to Atlanta, it failed. Keeping Forrest's forces occupied in the west meant that Sherman did not have to worry about a cavalry attacking from behind him or on his flank. Sherman sent a message to Colonel Hicks on April 3 regarding his defense of Paducah: "Your defense of Paducah was exactly right. Keep cool, and give the enemy a second edition if he comes again. I want Forrest to stay just where he is, and the longer the better."[209]

Chapter 6

Guerrilla Warfare and the Reign of Terror Under General Eleazer Paine

Guerrillas and the Governor

On January 4, 1864, the governor of Kentucky, Thomas E. Bramlette, issued a proclamation regarding the problem of the guerrilla attacks in Kentucky: "The frequent outrages perpetrated in various parts of the State by lawless bands of marauders can, in a large degree, be traced to the active aid of rebel sympathizers in our midst, or their neglect to furnish to military commandants the information in their possession, which would lead to the defeat and capture of such marauders." Bramlette requested all of the "various military commandants in the State of Kentucky will, in every instance where a loyal citizen is taken off by bands of guerrillas, immediately arrest at least five of the most prominent and active rebel sympathizers in the vicinity of such outrage for every loyal man taken by guerrillas. These sympathizers should be held as hostages for the safe and speedy return of the loyal citizens. Where there are disloyal relatives of guerrillas, they should be the chief sufferers. Let them learn that if they refuse to exert themselves actively for the assistance and protection of the loyal, they must expect to reap the just fruits of their complicity with the enemies of our State and people."[210]

After the Battle of Paducah

Throughout the war, guerrilla attacks in Kentucky were a constant problem, but after the Battle of Paducah, Federal military commanders in the region feared not only future attacks from the regular Confederate armies and cavalry but also the uptick of guerrilla activity in their areas. The Home Guard—Union men who volunteered to keep Kentucky safe in the hands of the Federals, who had been villainized by the secessionists in the region for their heavy-handed and lawless activities against them—ramped up their guerrilla warfare efforts in the region. Their aggressive tactics ensured revenge attacks against them, and with many guerrillas heartened with the arrival of General Forrest, this led to more and more attacks in the region.

One incident occurred after the Battle of Paducah that involved Confederate colonel Edward Crossland of the Seventh Kentucky Mounted Infantry. After Colonel Thompson was killed in Paducah, Crossland was next in line to take command of the attack on Fort Anderson, but he was shot in the thigh and forced from the field of battle. The next day, Crossland and a portion of his staff decided to spend the evening at the house of William Pryor, south of Mayfield, to rest for the evening before heading to Crossland's stepmother's property in Hickman, Kentucky.[211]

At about 9:00 p.m., Crossland was awakened by someone outside his window cursing, and when he yelled for them to go away, a shot came through the window. Soon after, the door burst open, and the leader began asking who they were. When one of Crossland's men replied that he was a rebel, he was shot in the chest. Crossland then heard, "You damn son-of-a-bitch in that bed, surrender," and he replied, "I am wounded and helpless, and of course I surrender." After this, he was shot at, but the bullet went beneath his armpit and hit the pillow—Crossland acted as if he were shot, yelled, "I am killed," and fell back as if he were dead. Crossland later learned that the man's name was Gregory, a well-known leader of the Home Guard in the area, and his group was known locally as Gregory's Cut-throats.[212]

Gregory's men attacked the rest of Crossland's men, leaving some dead and others injured as they ran to safety. Afterward, as it had quieted down, Crossland crawled out of bed to try to escape. Crawling out of the house, he hid in the chicken coop next to the house, with a wagon sheet over him to keep from freezing, but he feared being captured and killed if Gregory's men returned and burned down the house because the light would give him away. Crossland then crawled away from the house to a stake-and-

Unidentified soldier from Kentucky in Confederate uniform with two revolvers. *Library of Congress.*

ridered fence, but because of his wound and only wearing his nightclothes in the freezing cold, he was unable to get over the fence to get to safety. Fortunately for Crossland, one of his men was able to escape Gregory's men and find safety in the woods, and he saw Crossland struggling to get over the fence. He was able to carry Crossland on his back into the woods, but his man saw what he was wearing, so he went back to the house to find some bedclothes to cover him and returned to take care of his superior officer until the next morning, when a regiment of Confederate cavalry came from Mayfield and took them to safety back to that town. It was later said that Gregory took a uniform coat from one of Crossland's men who was shot and wore it on the streets of Paducah while riding Crossland's roan horse "with great parade and gusto."[213]

Because of all of the smuggling going on in the area to the Confederacy, General Mason Brayman, in Cairo, issued General Orders No. 15, on April 2, 1864, which stopped steamboats from landing in Paducah and Memphis, as well as all "ferry-boats, trading boats, skiffs, and other irregular craft." In it, he stated that "the large quantities of supplies which through permits (too freely granted), as well as by evasion of established regulations, have been carried into the interior of Western Kentucky, now partially under insurrectionary control, are now in the hands of the rebel forces affording them aid and comfort. Such supplies furnish an inducement to hostile incursion and support the marauders while making them, and it may be presumed that they were shipped and transported to the interior for the purpose of stopping the enemy's supplies."[214]

General Brayman also complained that goods were being transported by trains and disloyal citizens in western Kentucky to the Confederacy, and he wrote in one report, "On assuming command I found the railroad operated from Columbus to Union City, 26 miles, at the expense of the Government, and used to carry out supplies which went mostly into disloyal hands or were seized by Forrest. The road from Paducah to Mayfield was operated by its owners. Enormous quantities of supplies were carried to convenient points and passed into the hands of the rebel army…the disloyal citizens are open and avowed in their determination to kill, plunder, and expel from their homes all loyal men, and freely declare that none but such as sympathize with themselves shall take any party in the approaching elections."[215]

After the Battle of Paducah, General Forrest furloughed the Kentucky soldiers to visit their families, and after the men had time to rest and returned, Forrest learned that a number of fine horses were not found during their first time in Paducah, so he sent General Abraham Buford, with his Kentuckians, back to Paducah to take them to use in his cavalry, while Forrest was heading with the rest of his force to try to take Fort Pillow in western Tennessee on the Mississippi River. Buford arrived at Paducah on April 14, 1864, and when he threatened the city, Colonel Hicks again called his men into the fort to fight the invaders, as he had done on March 25. Buford did not try to attack the fort this time, and his raid was successful: he was able to retrieve two hundred horses from Paducah.[216]

Left: General John Hunt Morgan. *Library of Congress.*

Right: General Nathan Bedford Forrest, CSA. *Library of Congress.*

With both of Forrest's raids into western Kentucky in March and April, and with John Hunt Morgan's raids into central Kentucky in the first part of June, many of the rebel supporters felt bolstered to make many more attacks. In response to the regular Confederate army attacks and also the rebel guerrilla attacks, General Elihu B. Washburne, who was commanding western Kentucky and Tennessee, west of the Cumberland River, issued an order that stated that "the people of that disloyal region, Western Ky., will not be allowed to sell their cotton and tobacco, or purchase supplies, until they show some friendship for the U.S. government, by driving out the guerrillas and irregular bands of Confederate soldiers who pay them frequent visits."[217]

In response to all of the violent attacks in Kentucky, President Lincoln suspended the writ of habeas corpus and ordered martial law in Kentucky on July 5, 1864.[218]

GENERAL BURBRIDGE: THE BUTCHER OF KENTUCKY

In June 1864, General Stephen G. Burbridge was given command of the Department of Kentucky, and he wanted to stop all of the guerrilla activity that had been occurring. On July 16, 1864, Burbridge issued General Orders No. 59, which stated:

> *All guerrillas, armed prowlers, by whatever name they may be known, and rebel sympathizers are hereby admonished that in future stern retaliatory measures will be adopted and strictly enforced, whenever the lives or property of peaceful citizens are jeopardized by the lawless acts of such men. Rebel sympathizers living within five miles of any scene of outrage committed by armed men, not recognized as public enemies by the rules and usages of war, will be arrested and sent beyond the limits of the United States, in accordance with instructions from the major-general commanding the Military Division of the Mississippi." After the arrest of these individuals, the property of rebel sympathizers "as may be necessary to indemnify the Government or loyal citizens for losses incurred by the acts of such lawless men will be seized and appropriated for this purpose.*[219]

Burbridge went further by stating in the order that "whenever an unarmed Union citizen is murdered four guerrillas will be selected from the prisoners in the hands of the military authorities and publicly shot to death in the most convenient place near the scene of outrage."[220]

Even though these efforts were being used to try to stop rebel activity in Kentucky, they had a chilling effect on the population, whether they were unionist or secessionists alike, because with the suspension of habeas corpus and martial law being enacted, the rule of law was dictated according to whom was in command; if that person treated the citizens harshly and unfairly, they had little recourse to fight their actions.

GENERAL PAINE'S REIGN OF TERROR

With all of the illegal trade occurring inside and outside Paducah, the Union League of America members in the city wanted General Eleazer Paine reinstated to command in Paducah. They remembered when he was in command when Grant's forces took the city, and they knew that he would be harsh with the secessionists. They requested Paine's return in a letter to Major General C.C. Washburn on July 11, 1864:[221]

General Stephen G. Burbridge. NARA—526808. *Wikimedia Commons.*

ROOMS OF PADUCAH COUNCIL, No. 3,
UNION LEAGUE OF AMERICA,
Paducah, Ky., July 11, 1864

Maj. Gen. C.C. Washburn,
Commanding District of West Tennessee, Memphis, Tenn.:

SIR: We, the undersigned, officers of this council of the Union League of America, are requested by the council to write to you in reference to the present condition of affairs in this city. As the case now stands large quantities of goods of all descriptions are going from this post to the interior, and of course the articles find their way into the hands of rebels. Rebels are doing all the business, and they are reaping all the advantages of trade. The true Union men of this section of country were pleased with your former orders concerning trade, and we are satisfied in our own minds that if you were acquainted with the condition of affairs here, and could see the present workings of men who are now and ever have been enemies to the Government, you would at once bring about a change that would benefit the Union men and the Union cause. We have heard with pleasure the probability of our old and tried friend, General Paine, being assigned to command here and to have his headquarters in Paducah, and from him we hope and expect to obtain relief. We respectfully ask at your hands that you direct or permit General Paine to issue his orders relative to trade in Paducah according to his best judgment, believing as we do that he, being here upon the spot and being somewhat acquainted with the people here, will be able to protect Union men, and give traitors and secret Southern sympathizers their just dues. The members of this council of the Union League of America are residents of this Congressional district (First), consisting of fourteen counties. We have stood by our Union through weal and woe for the past three years of this terrible struggle, and we earnestly hope the military authorities will give us the protection we need and respectfully ask. Will you do us the honor to answer this communication, directing it to John Perkins, secretary, Paducah Council, No. 3, Union League of America.

We are, general, very respectfully, your obedient servants,
WM. H. KIDD,
President pro tempore.

THOMAS BARCHETT,
Vice-President.

JOHN PERKINS,
Secretary.

Honorable Cadwallader Colden Washburn. *Library of Congress.*

On July 19, 1864, General Paine was given command at Paducah, and it did not take long before Paine started directing his will to all of the citizens of the city. Paine made it known that only loyal people would be allowed to trade, and to carry out this trade policy, he levied a tax of ten dollars on every hogshead of tobacco or bale of cotton, with a tax assessment of 25 percent ad valorem on all cotton that had been owned by suspected disloyal citizens.[222]

On August 1, Paine instituted a tax of $100,000 on the residents in his military district from both suspected and known Confederate sympathizers. Beside this tax, Paine required heavy sums for all permits, and all bank checks could not be processed and paid unless approved by Paine or one of his agents—fifty cents for checks and ten cents for all letters, newspapers or packages, allowing them to leave Paducah. In some cases, Paine's own soldiers were charged from ten to fifty cents to mail a letter to their families.[223]

On August 8, General Paine banished citizens of Paducah to Canada, among them Mrs. Robert Woolfolk, along with her family, as well as other leading merchants and property owners of the city. After they were arrested, their goods were seized and guards were placed over them. Mrs. Woolfolk's husband, Robert, had been banished two weeks earlier, and many others chose to avoid arrest by escaping over to Illinois, out of Paine's command.[224]

On August 16, Brigadier General Henry Prince, commanding at Columbus, Kentucky, wanted nothing to do with Paine when he wrote to General Grant about Paine's command in western Kentucky:

> *The new policy propagates a new reign of terror by means of soldiers and hired assassins and unsettles every nook of society…This new commander took from my custody at Columbus, Ky., a man named Kesterson, whom I had captured and whom I was holding in prison for trial, conducted him to Paducah, Ky., and publicly killed him there, in semblance of an execution, without authority of law or any proper justification. One Gregory, a citizen heading a gang employed by the new commander and acting under his orders, took a man named Bryant from his bed, near Dublin, in the district, conducted him to Mayfield, and there publicly killed him in semblance of an execution, without authority of law or any proper justification…I beg leave, in vindication of myself, to add my protest against them in the name of God and of all my countrymen who respect the rights of mankind.*[225]

Eventually, reports of Paine's actions got back to Burbridge, and in response, he sent General Speed S. Frey and Colonel John Mason Brown as a commission to investigate the conduct of Paine and his subordinates. But when they arrived in Paducah on September 9, they discovered that Paine and his men had fled to Illinois, and with them went all of their records. General Solomon Meredith was given the command of Paducah when Paine left.[226]

General Frey and Colonel Brown continued their investigation, and they were told that Paine's favorite expression was, to men and women alike, "You are a God damned scoundrel; God damn you, I'll dig a hole and shoot and put you in it." They were told that private citizens were arrested and put into the guardhouse without any charges, and in one account, a Dr. Milan was confined for forty-one days and then released without knowing why he was there. Also, there were reports of executing suspected guerrillas without evidence, but there was not enough evidence to be found tying them back to Paine. Paine was ordered to return to Paducah in March 1865 to appear before a military court-martial for a formal trial, and many of the citizens of Paducah were upset when they learned that many of Paine's egregious crimes were omitted. After the war, the citizens of Paducah learned that the charges from Paine's indictment were dropped when a resolution in the U.S. Senate for arraignment was tabled and Paine only received a reprimand for his actions.[227]

Home Guard and Guerrillas

Due to the many complaints about the Home Guard and other Union-allied irregular forces, General Burbridge issued General Orders No. 3 on September 13: "The general commanding is pained to hear that, in various portions of his command, squads of Federal soldiers and companies of men styling themselves 'State Guards,' 'Home Guards,' 'Independent Companies,' &c., are roving over the country committing outrages on peaceable citizens, seizing without authority their horses and other property, insulting and otherwise maltreating them…But that any one, armed in the cause of Union and law, should engage in robbing and plundering defenseless citizens, is humiliating in the extreme, and he who so dishonors his calling deserves the severest punishment. Such outrages will not be tolerated longer, and the general commanding is determined, to the extent of his ability, to preserve law and order." He then instructed the officers under his command to enforce discipline against those disobeying the law.[228]

Regarding the rebel guerrillas, General Meredith in Paducah issued an appeal to the residents to meet at the Market House on October 18:[229]

> *Proclamation to the Citizens of Paducah.*
> *Headquarters District of Western Kentucky, Paducah, Ky., Oct. 18, 1864.*
>
> *The General commanding has information that the enemy who has before ravaged this district is threatening by his advance in the neighboring county to again attempt a raid of robbery and murder upon this place. In this crisis*

Guerrilla depredations: "Your money or your life!" Sketch by W.D. Matthews. *Library of Congress.*

he desires to call upon you to rally for your own defence. Your houses and firesides are in danger. You must defend them.

The General, therefore, appeals to every loyal citizen, capable of bearing arms, to lay aside all business and meet at 11 o'clock this (Tuesday) morning, in the market house, to organize and arm for the defence of the city. Immediately after the organization of companies of volunteers, arms and ammunition will be furnished by the officers assigned to that duty.

Patriots of Kentucky! You, whose sons stood shoulder to shoulder at Tippecanoe and on the red fields of Mexico, and bore through bloody strife the radiant flag of our glorious country—you are exhorted by all the sacred memories that stir the patriot's heart, to stand up once more for your fatherland. Show now, by free-will offering of yourselves, your loyalty and devotion to that Union under whose protection you owe all that you possess of wealth and honor, and whose foundations were made strong by the blood of your ancestors. Let the traitorous hordes of rebellion feel, if ever again they attempt their ruthless incursions upon your fair domains, that your loyal hearts and sturdy hands are pledged to deal swift vengeance upon them.

Left: General Solomon Meredith. NARA—526541. *Wikimedia Commons.*

Below: The Market House as it is in Paducah today. *Photo by author.*

The General commanding feels full confidence that he does not appeal to you in vain. The citizens of Paducah and Kentucky are still Americans and his countrymen, and he is assured that now, when an opportunity may be offered you to show your devotion to the flag, and brighten the record made glorious by your fathers, you will never desert that flag or disgrace that noble record.

S. Meredith,
Brig.-Gen. Com. District Western Kentucky.

The citizens of Paducah, and the region, were generally happy with the change to General Meredith because where Paine showed a lack of restraint and patience, Meredith became known for having a much more conciliatory policy toward the citizens of Paducah. To highlight this, one of Meredith's first acts was to empty the guardhouse in Paducah. In Mayfield, Kentucky, he released fifty-one people who were imprisoned there. The attack that Meredith feared never arrived, and eventually, the guerrilla attacks slowed after the main Confederate regular forces left the state. It would take a long time for the region to recover from all of the violence that continued from the irregular guerrilla activity. As the war went into its last year, Paducah and the region still endured hostile and violent acts caused by the years of guerrilla warfare in the region, to the detriment of its citizens.[230]

EPILOGUE

When the war finally ended, the lack of economic security in the region would take many years to finally recuperate, especially with the return of the soldiers who left to fight for both sides. Many of the people who operated businesses before the war did not have the means to continue, due to their losing everything they had. Many things in the Jackson Purchase had to begin anew.[231]

Because Kentucky was a slave state, and one that remained loyal to the Union in the war, slavery was not abolished right away. Eventually, with the institution of the Thirteenth Amendment in Kentucky, this led to the federal government maintaining a presence for years to come in the area with the Freedmen's Bureau, which lasted from December 1865 until 1872.[232]

However, Paducah still had the river trade and a connection to the Gulf of Mexico with the railroad, allowing trade and economic stability to finally return. Eventually, the animosities were largely left in the past, but parts of them can be seen even today in a lack of trust in the government for many people in the region—a lack of trust that has been maintained since the days of Andrew Jackson and his Jacksonian Democrats.

Notes

Chapter 1

1. Perrin, Battle and Kniffin, *Kentucky*, 106; Hoskins and Noe, *"Old First Is with the South,"* 32–33; Craig, "Kentucky's South Carolina," 28–34; Battle, Perrin and Kniffin, *Histories and Biographies of Ballard*, 4–5.
2. Shannon and McQuown, *Presidential Returns in Kentucky*, 1–3, 5–6; Hoskins and Noe, *"Old First Is with the South,"* 64–65.
3. Robertson and Robertson, *Paducah, Kentucky*, 23–24; Hoskins and Noe, *"Old First Is with the South,"* 65–67.
4. Robertson and Robertson, *Paducah, Kentucky*, 22; Hoskins and Noe, *"Old First Is with the South,"* 67–69.
5. Robertson and Robertson, *Paducah, Kentucky*; Hoskins and Noe, *"Old First Is with the South,"* 68–70.
6. Quigley, Langstaff and Langstaff, *Life & Times of Quintus Quincy Quigley*, 41–42.
7. Ibid.
8. Shannon and McQuown, *Presidential Returns in Kentucky*, 32–36; Craig, "Kentucky's South Carolina," 29–30; Perrin, Battle and Kniffin, *Kentucky*, 350.
9. Craig, "Kentucky's South Carolina," 28.
10. Quigley, Langstaff and Langstaff, *Life & Times of Quintus Quincy Quigley*, 61.
11. Ibid., 62.
12. Hoskins and Noe, *"Old First Is with the South,"* 83; Battle, Perrin and Kniffin, *Histories and Biographies of Ballard*, 81–82; Robertson, "Kentuckians Expelled by Federal Government," 116–34.

13. Robertson, "Kentuckians Expelled by Federal Government," 118–19; Quigley, Langstaff and Langstaff, *Life & Times of Quintus Quincy Quigley*, 69.
14. Quigley, Langstaff and Langstaff, *Life & Times of Quintus Quincy Quigley*, 69–70.
15. Excerpt from the *Paducah Herald* in the *Cairo City Weekly Gazette*, May 9, 1861; Craig, "Kentucky's Rebel Press," 20–27.
16. *Chicago Tribune* and *Kentucky Evening Post*, May 11, 1861; Moore, *Rebellion Record*, vol. 1, Doc. 139, 194.
17. Craig, "Kentucky's South Carolina," 31; *War of the Rebellion: A Compilation of the Official Records of the Union and Confederate Armies* (hereafter *OR*), ser. 1, vol. 52, pt. 2, 94; Craig, "Jackson Purchase Considers Secession," 339–61.
18. Craig, "Jackson Purchase Considers Secession," 339–47, 361; Craig, "Kentucky's South Carolina," 31–32.
19. *Memphis Appeal*, June 13, 1861; Russell, *My Diary, North and South*, 328; Craig, *Kentucky Confederates*, 95; Lee, *Civil War in the Jackson Purchase*, 40–41.
20. Russell, *My Diary, North and South*, 335–36; Craig, *Kentucky Confederates*, 95; Lee, *Civil War in the Jackson Purchase*, 40–41.
21. Kentucky, Federal Writers' Project, *Military History of Kentucky*, 89; Collins and Collins, *History of Kentucky*, vol. 1, 92; Lee, *Civil War in the Jackson Purchase*, 41.
22. George, *History of the 3d, 7th, 8th and 12th Kentucky*, 19; Kentucky, Federal Writers' Project, *Military History of Kentucky*, 89.
23. Craig, *Kentucky Confederates*, 95; Lee, *Civil War in the Jackson Purchase*, 40–41; Craig, "Northern Conquerors and Southern Deliverers," 17–30, 20–21; *OR*, vol. 4, 176–78.
24. Craig, "Northern Conquerors and Southern Deliverers," 20–21; Robertson and Robertson, *Paducah, Kentucky*, 28–29; Collins and Collins, *History of Kentucky*, vol. 1, 93; Quigley, Langstaff and Langstaff, *Life & Times of Quintus Quincy Quigley*, 71.

Chapter 2

25. *OR*, vol. 52, pt. 2, 61–62.
26. *Harper's Weekly*, June 1, 1861; *Memphis Daily Appeal*, April 26, 1861.
27. *OR*, vol. 52, pt. 2, 99; vol. 52, pt. 2, 100–101; vol. 52, pt. 2, 102–3.
28. Craig, "Northern Conquerors and Southern Deliverers," 19; Field and Hook, *American Civil War Fortifications*, 9.

29. *OR*, vol. 4, 376, 379.
30. Ibid., 381.
31. Collins and Collins, *History of Kentucky*, vol. 1, 92; Craig, *Kentucky Confederates*, 114.
32. *New York Times*, August 10, 1861.
33. *OR*, vol. 3, 685–87.
34. Collins and Collins, *History of Kentucky*, vol. 1, 92.
35. *OR*, vol. 3, 141–42; Grant and Simon, *Papers of Ulysses S. Grant*, vol. 2, 151.
36. *OR*, vol. 3, 142, 151–52; vol. 4, 180; Hughes, *Battle of Belmont*, 4.
37. *OR*, vol. 4, 179.
38. Ibid., vol. 3, 149.
39. Collins and Collins, *History of Kentucky*, vol. 1, 92; Grant and Simon, *Papers of Ulysses S. Grant*, vol. 2, 178.
40. *OR*, vol. 4, 181; Grant and Simon, *Papers of Ulysses S. Grant*, vol. 2, 178; *OR*, vol. 3, 148.
41. Grant and Simon, *Papers of Ulysses S. Grant*, vol. 2, 187.
42. *OR*, vol. 3, 148.
43. *OR*, vol. 4, 180–81.
44. Ibid., 180.
45. Grant and Simon, *Papers of Ulysses S. Grant*, vol. 2, 193; De Arnaud, *Union, and Its Ally, Russia*, 10–11.
46. *OR*, vol. 4, 196.
47. Grant and Long, *Personal Memoirs of U.S. Grant*, 80; *OR*, vol. 3, 150; vol. 4, 197.
48. *OR*, vol. 3, 149–50; Grant and Simon, *Papers of Ulysses S. Grant*, vol. 2, 191–92.
49. Grant and Simon, *Papers of Ulysses S. Grant*, vol. 2, 189–90; *OR*, vol. 3, 166.
50. Grant and Simon, *Papers of Ulysses S. Grant*, vol. 2, 196.
51. Moore, *Rebellion Record*, vol. 3, Doc. 31, 67; *OR*, vol. 4, 197.
52. *OR*, vol. 4, 197; Moore, *Rebellion Record*, vol. 3, Doc. 31, 67.
53. Grant and Long, *Personal Memoirs of U.S. Grant*, 215.
54. Grant and Simon, *Papers of Ulysses S. Grant*, vol. 2, 194–95.
55. *OR*, vol. 4, 197; Andreas, *History of Chicago*, vol. 2, 269–70.
56. *OR*, vol. 4, 198.
57. Grant and Simon, *Papers of Ulysses S. Grant*, vol. 2, 189; *OR*, vol. 52, pt.1, 189.
58. *OR*, vol. 3, 471, 149–50; Grant and Simon, *Papers of Ulysses S. Grant*, vol. 2, 198.
59. Grant and Simon, *Papers of Ulysses S. Grant*, vol. 2, 204; *Memphis Daily Appeal*, September 18, 1861.

60. Grant and Simon, *Papers of Ulysses S. Grant*, vol. 2, 205, 216.
61. Ibid., 205.
62. Moore, *Rebellion Record*, vol. 3, Doc. 31, 67–69.
63. *St. Louis Republican*, from the *Memphis Daily Appeal*, September 18, 1861.
64. *Louisville Courier*, September 12, 1861.
65. Wills and Kellogg, *Army Life of an Illinois Soldier*, 29.
66. *New York Times*, September 22, 1861; September 23, 1861; Collins and Collins, *History of Kentucky*, vol. 1, 96.
67. Merrill, Mastin and Miller, *Civil War Diary*, 2.
68. Grant and Long, *Personal Memoirs of U.S. Grant*, 80.
69. *OR*, vol. 4, 185–87.
70. Collins and Collins, *History of Kentucky*, vol. 1, 93; *New York Times*, September 26, 1861.
71. Collins and Collins, *History of Kentucky*, vol. 1, 93.

Chapter 3

72. Grant and Simon, *Papers of Ulysses S. Grant*, vol. 2, 205, 216; Catton, Bryant and Lewis, *Grant Moves South*, 50; Granger, *Military Order of the Loyal Legion*, vol. 5, 8.
73. *New York Times*, October 24, 1861.
74. *New York Times*, November 1, 1862; January 31, 1862.
75. Catton, Bryant and Lewis, *Grant Moves South*, 87; Morrison, *History of the Ninth Regiment*, 15; *United States Army and Navy Journal*, vol. 2, *Recollections of the Fallen—July 8, 1865*, 722; *OR*, vol. 8, 408–10.
76. *Report of the Proceedings of the Society of the Army of the Tennessee at the Thirty-sixth Meeting Held at Council Bluff, Iowa, November 8–9, 1906*, 92–93; Catton, Bryant and Lewis, *Grant Moves South*, 87.
77. *OR*, vol. 3, 471, 149–50; vol. 52, pt. 1, 189; Grant and Simon, *Papers of Ulysses S. Grant*, vol. 2, 5, 189, 198; Chetlain, *Recollections of Seventy Years*, 83.
78. *OR*, vol. 4, 302; Lee, *Civil War in the Jackson Purchase*, 73–74.
79. Wallace, *Lew Wallace*, 351–53.
80. *OR*, vol. 3, 299–300; Catton, Bryant and Lewis, *Grant Moves South*, 80; Lee, *Civil War in the Jackson Purchase*, 74.
81. *OR*, vol. 3, 299–300, 302; Catton, Bryant and Lewis, *Grant Moves South*, 80; Lee, *Civil War in the Jackson Purchase*, 74–75.
82. *OR*, vol. 3, 303.

83. Allen, *Center of Conflict*, 29.
84. Ibid.
85. *Paducah Sun*, February 23, 1905.
86. *New York Times*, December 8, 1861; Durham and Patrick, *Three Years with Wallace's Zouaves*, 60–61; *Chicago Tribune*, December 3, 1861.
87. *Chicago Tribune*, December 3, 1861.
88. Moore, *Rebellion Record*, vol. 3. Doc. 190, 418.
89. Wallace, *Lew Wallace*, 351.
90. *Chicago Tribune*, December 3, 1861.
91. *Cincinnati Commercial*, December 5, 1861.
92. Catton, Bryant and Lewis, *Grant Moves South*, 88.
93. Grant and Simon, *Papers of Ulysses S. Grant*, vol. 3, xxv, 332.

Chapter 4

94. *OR*, vol. 17, pt. 2, 424.
95. Robertson and Robertson, *Paducah, Kentucky*, 41; Sarna, *When General Grant*, 3–4.
96. Sarna, *When General Grant*, 3–4; Ash, *Civil War Exodus*, 515.
97. Sarna, *When General Grant*, 5–6; Ash, *Civil War Exodus*, 515.
98. Sarna, *When General Grant*; Ash, *Civil War Exodus*, 514–15.
99. *Official Records of the Union and Confederate Navies in the War of the Rebellion Washington: Government Printing Office* (hereafter *OR Navies*), 1908, vol. 22, 479.
100. Ash, *Civil War Exodus*, 506.
101. Ibid., 507.
102. Ibid.
103. Ibid., 508.
104. Sherman and Howe, *Home Letters of General Sherman*, 229–30.
105. Ash, *Civil War Exodus*, 508; *OR*, vol. 52, pt. 1, 331; Dana, *Recollections of the Civil War*, 18.
106. *OR*, vol. 17, pt. 2, 421.
107. Ibid.
108. Ash, *Civil War Exodus*, 508.
109. Grant and Simon, *Papers of Ulysses S. Grant*, vol. 6, 283; Dana, *Recollections of the Civil War*, 17.
110. Sarna, *When General Grant*, 47–48.
111. Ash, *Civil War Exodus*, 511; Wilson, *Life of John A. Rawlins*, 96.

112. Sarna, *When General Grant*, 18–19.
113. *Israelite*, January 23, 1863, 229; Ash, *Civil War Exodus*, 513.
114. Sarna, *When General Grant*, 8; *OR*, vol. 17, pt. 2, 463; Ash, *Civil War Exodus*, 513; Cadwallader and Thomas, *Three Years with Grant*, 34–40.
115. Cadwallader and Thomas, *Three Years with Grant*, 34–40; Ash, *Civil War Exodus*, 513.
116. Sarna, *When General Grant*, 18; Jewish American History Foundation, Philip Trounstine to Major C.S. Hayes.
117. Ash, *Civil War Exodus*, 512; Jewish American History Foundation, "How General Grant's Order Did Work."
118. Ash, *Civil War Exodus*, 513–14; Sarna, *When General Grant*s, 6.
119. Sarna, *When General Grant*, 6.
120. Ibid.
121. *OR*, vol. 17, pt. 2, 506; Sarna, *When General Grant*, 8–9.
122. Miller, *War and Peace of Mind*, 40; Grant and Simon, *Papers of Ulysses S. Grant*, vol. 7, 55; *OR*, vol. 17, pt. 2, 506.
123. Ash, *Civil War Exodus*, 514; Robertson and Robertson, *Paducah, Kentucky*, 42.
124. Sarna, *When General Grant*, 12; Markens, *Abraham Lincoln and the Jews*, 118; Sarna, "General Grant's Infamous Order."
125. Sarna, *When General Grant*, 12–13.
126. Ash, *Civil War Exodus*, 518.
127. Markens, *Abraham Lincoln and the Jews*, 118; Miller, *War and Peace of Mind*, 40; Sarna, *When General Grant*, 21; Ash, *Civil War Exodus*, 518.
128. Ash, *Civil War Exodus*, 518; Markens, *Abraham Lincoln and the Jews*, 118.
129. Markens, *Abraham Lincoln and the Jews*, 118; Ash, *Civil War Exodus*, 518; Sarna, *When General Grant*, 21.
130. *OR*, vol. 17, pt. 2, 530; Ash, *Civil War Exodus*, 518; Grant and Simon, *Papers of Ulysses S. Grant*, vol. 7, 53.
131. Sarna, *When General Grant*, 22; Markens, *Abraham Lincoln and the Jews*, 119.
132. Grant and Simon, *Papers of Ulysses S. Grant*, vol. 7, 54; Ash, *Civil War Exodus*, 519.
133. *OR*, vol. 17, pt. 2, 544; Grant and Simon, *Papers of Ulysses S. Grant*, vol. 7, 54; *OR*, vol. 24, pt. 1, 9.
134. McClure, *Abraham Lincoln and Men of War-Times*, 193–96.
135. Markens, *Abraham Lincoln and the Jews*, 119; Ash, *Civil War Exodus*, 518; Sarna, *When General Grant*, 22–23.
136. Sarna, *When General Grant*, 22–23; *Israelite*, January 16, 1863, 218; Markens, *Abraham Lincoln and the Jews*, 119–20; Ash, *Civil War Exodus*, 519.

137. *Congressional Globe*, 37th Cong., 3rd sess., January 9, 1863, part 1, 245; *Israelite*, January 16, 1863, 218; Markens, *Abraham Lincoln and the Jews*, 120.
138. *New York Times*, "Grant and the Jews," June 22, 1868; Sarna, "General Grant's Infamous Order"; Sarna, *When General Grant*, xi, introduction.
139. Sarna, "General Grant's Infamous Order"; Sarna, *When General Grant*, 49; Simon, *Personal Memoirs of Julia Dent Grant*, 107.
140. Sarna, "General Grant's Infamous Order."

Chapter 5

141. Collins and Collins, *History of Kentucky*, vol. 1, 127; Robertson and Robertson, *Paducah, Kentucky*, 38–39.
142. Jennie Fyfe to Nell Fyfe, Fyfe Family Papers, March 20, 1864.
143. Perrin, Battle and Kniffin, *Kentucky*, 83.
144. *OR*, vol. 32, pt. 3, 131.
145. Ibid., pt. 1, 628.
146. George, *History of the 3d, 7th, 8th and 12th Kentucky*, 78.
147. Robertson and Robertson, *Paducah, Kentucky*, 44, 46.
148. *OR*, vol. 32, pt. 3, p. 144.
149. Jennie Fyfe Letters, March 20, 1864.
150. Perrin, Battle and Kniffin, *Kentucky*, 83.
151. Jennie Fyfe Letters, March 20, 1864.
152. Ibid., April 6, 1864.
153. *OR*, vol. 32, pt. 1, 551.
154. *OR*, vol. 32, pt. 1, 548; Hoskins and Noe, *"Old First Is with the South,"* 173; Huch, "Fort Pillow Massacre," 62–70; *Fort Anderson, Paducah, Kentucky*, John Rziha illustration, 1861. On bottom of illustration, the scale is twenty feet to one inch, so four hundred by four hundred feet.
155. *OR*, vol. 32, pt. 1, 549; Robertson and Robertson, *Paducah, Kentucky*, 44.
156. Jennie Fyfe Letters, April 6, 1864.
157. *Estate of Dr. J.M. Best, deceased, v. The United States, Sam Houston*, 2.
158. Jennie Fyfe Letters, April 6, 1864.
159. Ibid.
160. Ibid.
161. Ibid.
162. Ibid.
163. Ibid.
164. *OR*, vol. 32, pt. 1, 551.

165. Ibid., 547; Huch, "Civil War Letters of Herbert Saunders," 17–29.
166. Neuman, *Paducahans in History*, 58.
167. George, *History of the 3d, 7th, 8th and 12th Kentucky*, 76; Neuman, *Paducahans in History*, 59.
168. *OR Navies*, vol. 26, 199–200.
169. *OR*, vol. 32, pt. 1, 551; *OR Navies*, vol. 26, 199–200.
170. Neuman, *Paducahans in History*, 58, 60; Perrin, Battle and Kniffin, *Kentucky*, 83; *OR Navies*, vol. 26, 201.
171. *OR*, vol. 32, pt. 1, 547, 551; Perrin, Battle and Kniffin, *Kentucky*, 83; *OR Navies*, vol. 26, 201.
172. Neuman, *Paducahans in History*, 60; George, *History of the 3d, 7th, 8th and 12th Kentucky*, 76; *OR Navies*, vol. 26, 199–200.
173. George, *History of the 3d, 7th, 8th and 12th Kentucky*, 76.
174. Neuman, *Paducahans in History*, 64–65.
175. Ibid. 61; *OR*, vol. 32, pt. 1, 547; *OR Navies*, vol. 26, 201.
176. Huch, "Civil War Letters of Herbert Saunders," 23.
177. Moore, *Rebellion Record*, vol. 8, 506.
178. Ibid.
179. *OR Navies*, vol. 26, 199–200.
180. Neuman, *Paducahans in History*, 62–63; *OR*, vol. 32, pt. 1, 547, 551; Grief, "General Forrest's Raid on Paducah," 212–13.
181. George, *History of the 3d, 7th, 8th and 12th Kentucky*, 76; Neuman, *Paducahans in History*, 63; Perrin, Battle and Kniffin, *Kentucky*, 89; Grief, "General Forrest's Raid on Paducah," 212–13.
182. *OR*, vol. 32, pt. 1, 547.
183. Ibid., 551.
184. Neuman, *Paducahans in History*, 63; Grief, "General Forrest's Raid on Paducah," 212–13.
185. *OR*, vol. 32, pt. 1, 551.
186. Neuman, *Paducahans in History*, 64.
187. George, *History of the 3d, 7th, 8th and 12th Kentucky*, 76; Neuman, *Paducahans in History*, 64.
188. *OR Navies*, vol. 26, 199–200; *OR*, vol. 32, pt. 1, 547.
189. Jennie Fyfe Letters, April 6, 1864.
190. Ibid.
191. Ibid.
192. Robertson, *Paducah*, 48.
193. Moore, *Rebellion Record*, vol. 8, 499–501.
194. Neuman, *Paducahans in History*, 68.

195. *OR*, vol. 32, pt. 1, 548.
196. George, *History of the 3d, 7th, 8th and 12th Kentucky*, 78.
197. *OR*, vol. 32, pt. 1, 548.
198. Ibid.
199. Neuman, *Paducahans in History*, 67.
200. Ibid., 70.
201. Moore, *Rebellion Record*, vol. 8, 499–501.
202. Jennie Fyfe Letters, April 6, 1864.
203. Robertson and Robertson, *Paducah, Kentucky*, 46; *OR*, vol. 32, pt. 1, 547.
204. George, *History of the 3d, 7th, 8th and 12th Kentucky*, 77.
205. Robertson and Robertson, *Paducah, Kentucky*, 46.
206. Ibid.
207. George, *History of the 3d, 7th, 8th and 12th Kentucky*, 77; Robertson and Robertson, *Paducah, Kentucky*, 46.
208. Robertson and Robertson, *Paducah, Kentucky*, 46.
209. *OR*, vol. 32, pt. 3, 242.

Chapter 6

210. *New York Times*, January 17, 1864.
211. George, *History of the 3d, 7th, 8th and 12th Kentucky*, 79.
212. Ibid; Whitesell, "Military Operations in the Jackson Purchase Area," 240–67.
213. George, *History of the 3d, 7th, 8th and 12th Kentucky*, 79–81.
214. *OR*, vol. 32, pt. 1, 514–15.
215. Ibid., 512.
216. George, *History of the 3d, 7th, 8th and 12th Kentucky*, 78; Robertson and Robertson, *Paducah, Kentucky*, 47–48; Barton, "Civil War in the Purchase," 79–91.
217. Robertson and Robertson, *Paducah, Kentucky*, 48; Collins and Collins, *History of Kentucky*, vol. 1, 134.
218. Collins and Collins, *History of Kentucky*, vol. 1, 135; Robertson and Robertson, *Paducah, Kentucky*, 48.
219. *OR*, vol. 39, pt. 2, 174; *New York Times*, July 23, 1864.
220. *OR*, vol. 39, pt. 2, 174; *New York Times*, July 23, 1864.
221. *OR*, vol. 39, pt. 2, 171.
222. Ibid., 144; Kerr, Connelley and Coulter, *History of Kentucky*, 880; *Kentucky Senate Journals*, 1865, 27.

223. Collins and Collins, *History of Kentucky*, vol. 1, 138; Robertson and Robertson, *Paducah, Kentucky*, 48; Kerr, Connelley and Coulter, *History of Kentucky*, 880.
224. Collins and Collins, *History of Kentucky*, vol. 1, 138; Robertson and Robertson, *Paducah, Kentucky*, 48.
225. *OR*, vol. 39, pt. 2, 260–61; Grant and Simon, *Papers of Ulysses S. Grant*, vol. 12, 124–25.
226. Collins and Collins, *History of Kentucky*, vol. 1, 140.
227. *Kentucky Senate Journals*, 1865, 25–27; Collins and Collins, *History of Kentucky*, vol. 1, 140; *Journal of the Senate of the United States*, December 5, 1864, 109; Barton, "Reign of Terror in Graves County," 493, 495.
228. *OR*, vol. 39, pt. 2, 375; Collins and Collins, *History of Kentucky*, vol. 1, 141.
229. *New York Times*, October 23, 1864.
230. Robertson and Robertson, *Paducah, Kentucky*, 50.

Epilogue

231. Robertson and Robertson, *Paducah, Kentucky*, 51.
232. Kerr, Connelley and Coulter, *History of Kentucky*, vol. 2, 912; Robertson and Robertson, *Paducah, Kentucky*, 52.

Bibliography

Books

Allen, Hall. *Center of Conflict: A Factual Story of the War Between the States in Western Kentucky and Tennessee*. Paducah, KY: Paducah Sun-Democrat, 1961.

Andreas, A.T. *History of Chicago: From the Earliest Period to the Present Time*. Chicago: self-published, 1885.

Ash, Stephen V. *Civil War Exodus: The Jews and Grant's General Orders No. 11*. Allentown, PA: Phi Alpha Theta International Honor Society in History, 1982.

Battle, J.H., William Henry Perrin and G.C. Kniffin. *Histories and Biographies of Ballard, Calloway, Fulton, Graves, Hickman, McCracken and Marshall Counties, Kentucky*. Murray: Kentucky Reprint, 1972.

Cadwallader, Sylvanus, and Benjamin Platt Thomas. *Three Years with Grant*. New York: Knopf, 1955.

Catton, Bruce, Samuel H. Bryant and Lloyd Lewis. *Grant Moves South*. Boston: Little, Brown, 1960.

Chetlain, Augustus L. *Recollections of Seventy Years*. Galena, IL: Gazette Pub., 1899.

Collins, Lewis, and Richard H. Collins. *History of Kentucky*. Vol. 1. Covington, KY: Collins & Company, 1882.

Craig, Berry. *Kentucky Confederates: Secession, Civil War, and the Jackson Purchase*. Lexington: University of Kentucky Press, 2014.

Dana, Charles A. *Recollections of the Civil War: With the Leaders at Washington and in the Field in the Sixties*. New York: D. Appleton and Company, 1898.

De Arnaud, Charles A. *The Union, and Its Ally, Russia: An Historical Narrative of the Most Critical and Exciting Period of Our Late War, Reminiscences*. Washington, D.C.: Gibson Bros., Printers and Bookbinders, 1890.

Durham, Thomas W., and Jeffrey L. Patrick. *Three Years with Wallace's Zouaves: The Civil War Memoirs of Thomas Wise Durham*. Macon, GA: Mercer University Press, 2003.

Field, Ron, and Adam Hook. *American Civil War Fortifications (3): The Mississippi and River Forts*. Oxford, NY: Osprey, 2007.

George, Henry. *History of the 3d, 7th, 8th and 12th Kentucky C.S.A*. Louisville, KY: C.T. Dearing, 1911.

Granger, James N. *Military Order of the Loyal Legion of the United States, Minnesota Commandery: Companion Warren Granger, Lieutenant-Colonel 100th N.Y. Infantry and Brevet Colonel U.S. Volunteers*. Hartford, CT: Press of the Case, Lockwood & Brainard, 1895.

Grant, Ulysses S., and E.B. Long. *Personal Memoirs of U.S. Grant*. New York: Da Capo Press, 1982.

Grant, Ulysses S., and John Y. Simon. *The Papers of Ulysses S. Grant*. Carbondale: Southern Illinois University, 1977.

Hoskins, Patricia Ann., and Kenneth W. Noe. *"The Old First Is with the South": The Civil War, Reconstruction, and Memory in the Jackson Purchase Region of Kentucky*. Auburn, AL: Auburn University, 2009.

Hughes, Nathaniel Cheairs. *The Battle of Belmont: Grant Strikes South*. Chapel Hill: University of North Carolina Press, 1991.

Kentucky, Federal Writers' Project. *Military History of Kentucky*. Frankfort, KY: printed by the State Journal, 1939.

Kerr, Charles, William Elsey Connelley and E. Merton Coulter. *History of Kentucky*. Chicago: American Historical Society, 1922.

Lee, Dan. *The Civil War in the Jackson Purchase, 1861–1862: The Pro-Confederate Struggle and Defeat in Southwest Kentucky*. Jefferson, NC: McFarland, 2014.

Markens, Isaac. *Abraham Lincoln and the Jews*. New York: printed for the author, 1909.

McClure, Alexander. *Abraham Lincoln and Men of War-Times: Some Personal Recollections of War and Politics during the Lincoln Administration*. Philadelphia: Times Publishing Company, 1892.

Merrill, Carole, Aaron Loder Mastin and Viola Jane Mastin Miller. *The Civil War Diary (transcribed) of Aaron Loder Mastin*. Las Vegas, NV: C. Merrill, 1999.

Miller, Caryn. *War and Peace of Mind: The Jewish Expulsion and the Election of President Ulysses S. Grant*. New Brunswick, NJ: Rutgers University Press, 2011.

Moore, Frank. *The Rebellion Record: A Diary of American Events, with Documents, Narratives, Illustrative Incidents, Poetry, Etc.* Vol. 1. New York: D. Van Nostrand, 1865.

Morrison, Marion. *A History of the Ninth Regiment, Illinois Volunteer Infantry.* Monmouth, IL: J.S. Clark, Printer, 1864.

Neuman, Fred Gus. *Paducahans in History.* Paducah, KY: Young Print., 1922.

Official Records of the Union and Confederate Navies in the War of the Rebellion. Washington, D.C.: Government Printing Office, 1908.

Perrin, William Henry, J.H. Battle and G.C. Kniffin. *Kentucky: A History of the State.* Louisville, KY: F.A. Battey, 1888.

Quigley, Quintus Quincy, George Quigley Langstaff and Maureen Black Langstaff. *The Life & Times of Quintus Quincy Quigley, 1828–1910: His Personal Journal, 1859–1908.* Paducah, KY: Paducah Area Community Foundation, 1999.

Report of the Proceedings of the Society of the Army of the Tennessee at the Thirty-Sixth Meeting Held at Council Bluff, Iowa, November 8–9, 1906. Cincinnati, OH: Chas. O. Ebel Printing Company, 1907.

Robertson, John. *Paducah: Frontier to the Atomic Age.* Charleston, SC: Arcadia Publishing, 2002.

Robertson, John E.L., and Ann E. Robertson. *Paducah, Kentucky: A History.* Charleston, SC: The History Press, 2014.

Russell, William Howard. *My Diary, North and South.* New York: Harper, 1863.

Sarna, Jonathan D. *When General Grant Expelled the Jews.* New York: Nextbook, 2012.

Shannon, Jasper, and Ruth McQuown. *Presidential Returns in Kentucky: A Compilation of Election Statistics and an Analysis of Political Behavior.* Lexington: University of Kentucky Bureau of Government Research, 1950.

Sherman, William T., and M.A. De Wolfe Howe. *Home Letters of General Sherman.* New York: C. Scribner's Sons, 1909.

Simon, John. *The Personal Memoirs of Julia Dent Grant.* Carbondale: Southern Illinois University Press, 1975.

United States Army and Navy Journal. Vol. 2, *Recollections of the Fallen—July 8, 1865.* Carbondale: Southern Illinois University Press, 1975.

Wallace, Lew. *Lew Wallace: An Autobiography.* New York: Harper & Brothers, 1906.

War of the Rebellion: A Compilation of the Official Records of the Union and Confederate Armies. Washington, D.C.: Government Printing Office, 1871.

Wills, Charles Wright, and Mary E. Kellogg. *Army Life of an Illinois Soldier: Including a Day-by-Day Record of Sherman's March to the Sea: Letters and Diary of Charles W. Wills*. Carbondale: Southern Illinois University Press, 1996.
Wilson, James Harrison. *The Life of John A. Rawlins, Lawyer, Assistant Adjutant-General, Chief of Staff, Major General of Volunteers, and Secretary of War*. New York: Neale Pub., 1916.

Government Documents

Journal of the Senate of the United States. 1864.
Kentucky Senate Journals. 1865.

Articles

Barton, Lon Carter. "The Civil War in the Purchase." *Journal of the Jackson Purchase Historical Society* 17 (1990): 79–91.
———. "The Reign of Terror in Graves County." *Register of the Kentucky Hstorical Society* 46, no. 155 (April 1948): 493, 495.
Craig, Berry. "The Jackson Purchase Considers Secession: The 1861 Mayfield Convention." *Register of the Kentucky Historical Society* 99, no. 4 (2001): 28–34.
———. "Kentucky's Rebel Press: The Jackson Purchase Newspapers in 1861." *Register of the Kentucky Historical Society* 75, no. 1 (1977): 20–27.
———. "Kentucky's South Carolina: The Jackson Purchase in the Secession Crisis of 1860–1861." *Journal of the Jackson Purchase Historical Society* 3 (1976): 28–34.
———. "Northern Conquerors and Southern Deliverers: The Civil War Comes to the Jackson Purchase." *Register of the Kentucky Historical Society* 73, no. 1 (1975): 17–30.
Huch, Ronald K. "The Civil War Letters of Herbert Saunders." *Register of the Kentucky Historical Society* 69, no. 1 (January 1971): 17–29.
———. "Fort Pillow Massacre: The Aftermath of Paducah." *Illinois State Historical Society Journal* 66 (Spring 1973): 62–70.
Jewish American History Foundation. "How General Grant's Order Did Work Before It Was Revoked." http://www.jewish-history.com/civilwar/go11.htm.
———. Philip Trounstine to Major C.S. Hayes, Moscow, Tennessee, March 3, 1863. http://www.jewish-history.com/civilwar/trnstine.htm.

Robertson, John. "Kentuckians Expelled by Federal Government." *Jackson Purchase Historical Society Journal* 40 (2013): 116–34.

Sarna, Jonathan D. "General Grant's Infamous Order." *New York Times*, December 19, 2012.

Whitesell, Hunter. "Military Operations in the Jackson Purchase Area of Kentucky, 1862–1851 (Part 2)." *Register of the Kentucky Historical Society* 63, no. 3 (1965): 240–67.

Periodicals

Confederate Veteran. 1897.

Congressional Globe. 37th Cong, 3rd sess., January 9, 1863.

Harper's Weekly. June 1, 1861.

Newspapers

Cairo City Weekly Gazette.

Chicago Tribune.

Cincinnati Commercial.

Israelite.

Louisville Courier.

Memphis Appeal.

Memphis Daily Appeal.

New York Times.

Paducah Sun.

St. Louis Republican.

Collections

Estate of Dr. J.M. Best, deceased, v. The United States, Sam Houston. Library of Congress, call no. 5930312.

Jennie Fyfe to Nell Fyfe, March 20, 1864. Fyfe Family Papers. Special Collections, Bentley Historical Library, University of Michigan, Ann Arbor, Michigan. From the collection of the McCracken County Public Library Special Collections.

Rziha, John. *Fort Anderson, Paducah, Kentucky.* Illustration, 1861. Library of Congress Geography and Map Division, Washington, D.C. 20540-4650 USA dcu, catalogue no. 2008627280.

Index

D

E

F

G

H

J

K

L

M

N

O

P

Q

R

S

T

U

V

W

About the Author

John Cashon's family moved to the Dukedom, Kentucky area in the Jackson Purchase of Kentucky and Tennessee in 1824 after his fifth-great-grandfather David Cashon received a Revolutionary War Land Grant for his service as a minuteman in Chesterfield, Virginia, while serving under General Lafayette before and during the Siege of Yorktown when Cornwallis surrendered. John's family then moved to Feliciana, Kentucky, in 1847; his second-great-grandfather Jerome Washington Cashon was thirteen years old when the Civil War began. He lived within a mile of Camp Beauregard, used by the Confederate army early in the war.

John also had a family member who fought in the war. His second-great grandfather Ephraim Davenport Osburn was a Confederate soldier from Canton, Kentucky, in the Eighth Kentucky Infantry, Company B, which later became the Eighth Kentucky Mounted Infantry under the command of General Nathan Bedford Forrest.

John went to high school at Paducah Tilghman, named after Augusta Tilghman, the wife of Confederate brigadier general Lloyd Tilghman. He received his bachelor's degree in history at Murray State University. Because his father was a great storyteller, it sparked his interests in local history. This played a prominent role in why it was important for him to begin writing histories.